Growing Up With The Trees

A Shepparton Story

Aaron Feiglin

makor
Jewish
Community
Library

The 'Write Your Story' Collection

Published by Makor Jewish Community Library
306 Hawthorn Road
Caulfield South
Victoria 3162
Australia

ISBN   1 876733 79 9

Production: Inklink Advertising Pty Ltd
Tel: (03) 9528 2056

Cover design by Izi Marmur from Izigraphics Pty Ltd

WRITE YOUR STORY is a cultural activity of Makor Jewish Community Library. It is facilitated by Julie Meadows.

It is to my dear wife, children, grandchildren and great-grandchildren that I dedicate this story

Acknowledgements

Having worked on my memory to produce all that I have written, I sit back and reflect that this would not have happened if my dear wife had not encouraged me and pushed me with it. So, to her I give all my love and thanks. I thank her not only for her encouragement, but for her kindness to me and our children, and as time went on, to our grandchildren and now to our great-grandchildren who, without exception, love her dearly. Their acceptance of our way of life as strictly observant Jews has given me more happiness and joy than I ever imagined possible.

I would like to thank Julie Meadows, the co-ordinator of the Makor Library's Write Your Story Program, for giving me the opportunity to publish my story and Izi and Eti Marmur for transforming it into this book.

Last but not least, I must add a very special thanks to Ruth Mushin, who soon learnt to decipher my bad writing and did all the typing and editing. As Ruth has reminded me, if my late mother had not cared for her late father in Metullah so many years ago – a story you will read in my book – this may not have been possible.

Unless explained in the text, words that appear in italics are defined in the glossary at the end of the book.

Contents

Introduction

I have named this little book *Growing up with the Trees*. I could have, or maybe should have, called it *Hamalach hagoil oisi mikol ror* (The Angel Who Keeps Me from Everything Bad) – you will see why as you read further. This book, although giving an insight into how it was to be on the orchards, must necessarily touch on many topics, be it about the farm animals and other things you will find on an orchard, such as horses, dogs, cows, fowls and even a cat.

From Metullah via Melbourne to Shepparton

My paternal and maternal grandparents came from Russia, both families coming to Palestine (now Israel) in the late nineteenth century to escape the pogroms in Russia.

My paternal grandfather, Yaakov Zvi, was the son of Abraham, the son of Nachum. Rev Abraham lived to ninety years old. Yaakov Zvi was born in 1848. His wife, Elisheva, as was told, was a tall, very beautiful woman, who passed away in 1883 at the age of thirty-three. Moshe Zalman Feiglin, my father, was born in Gorky, Russia, in 1875.

Yaakov Zvi decided to go to Palestine and take the younger members of the family with him, to escape the pogroms. He was happy to leave his worldly possessions behind, as long as he could get out with his family. Originally Yaakov Zvi settled on the land in Rishon LeZion, but was talked into exchanging his land there for land in Mishmar Hayarden in the north. After years of back-breaking work to clear the land of rocks, and ill health caused by navigating the swamps, my father and his older brother, Shmuel, quit the land. They first found jobs building roads and later worked in the first vineyards established in Zirkon Yaakov by Baron Hirsch Rothschild. My father was then promoted to delivering wages to all the vineyards Baron Rothschild had established in Palestine. He would ride from vineyard to vineyard on horseback.

Shmuel settled in Metullah and one day, when Moshe Zalman went to visit him, Shmuel introduced him to Leah, the daughter of Shaye and Pearl Abramovitch. Leah, my mother, was born in 1885 in Lithuania, thirteen years after her parents' marriage, when they had given up hope of having a child. The family came to Palestine when Leah was a small girl.

My mother would tell us stories about life in Lithuania and one of my favourites was about the turkeys they had. They made wine out of raisins and would then throw the raisins out in the yard. The turkeys had a great feast, but ended up drunk on the ground. Thinking they had been killed, the maid plucked them all and soon enough, lots of naked turkeys were running around. In haste, the family collected all the old wool they could find in the village to knit 'jackets' for the turkeys to save them from freezing!

Many European Jews trekked by foot through Turkey, Syria and Lebanon to Palestine, risking attacks, malnutrition and all else that could befall one on such a journey. They finally arrived in Metullah, on the Lebanese border. My maternal grandparents had settled in Metullah and would attend to the needs of other Jewish people who came via this route, housing them and nursing them back to health. So many people passed through this route that the house of my grandparents was named 'Shayke's Hotel'.

Pearl was a woman who liked things to be just right and was so efficient that she had very little housework for my mother to do. As there were other families who needed help, Pearl would send her daughter from house to house to lend a hand, which she continued to do for the rest of her life.

Moshe Zalman and Leah were married in 1900, when my

father was twenty-three and my mother was sixteen. They settled in Metullah and their first child, Abraham, was born in 1901. Next came Judah, Joseph, Zipporah (known as Bertha) and Modche (later Mark).

In 1911, as my father did his rounds of Baron Rothschild's vineyards, he found out that the army of the Ottoman Empire was conscripting soldiers to fight its wars. They had broken into the homes of settlers in nearby Rosh Pinnah and were on their way to Metullah. As soon as my father got wind of this, he packed his saddlebags and left. It was almost a split-second decision as he did not want to become canon fodder for the Ottoman Empire.

My father rode to Beirut and then on to Port Said, arriving there just before *Rosh Hashannah* and *Yom Kippur*. He went along to the *shul*, where the congregation had hired a man who came from Cairo to lead the services. On *Rosh Hashannah*, this man said that it was too much for him to lead the entire service and blow the *shofar* and asked if there was anyone willing to help him. My father volunteered and started the *davening*. My father had a very sweet tenor voice and prayed with great sincerity and at the end of the first part of the service, the congregation wouldn't let him leave. They asked him to continue but my father refused saying, 'You've hired a man. I don't want to take away his *parnosse*!' Years later, my father was walking down Drummond Street in Carlton when he heard a girl call out, 'Mama, Mama, *dort geit* (there goes) the Port Said *chazen*!'

My father's younger brother, Bere, had gone to Australia and his brother, Izik, had gone to the United States of America. As my father waited for a ship in Port Said, he decided to get on whichever ship came first, whether it was going to America,

Australia or wherever. The first ship that docked happened to be going to Australia, so that's where he went!

When my father arrived in Melbourne, he found a job in Collingwood washing bottles. His wage was 14/6 ($1.45) per week. On Friday night and Saturday, he didn't turn up for work, so the boss asked him why. My father replied that Friday night and Saturday were his *Shabbos*, which was a time of rest. As the boss said he could only pay my father half wages for the time he had worked, he decided to leave. He continued to work at menial jobs, repeatedly being fired after not turning up to work on *Shabbos*.

In 1913, about a year after my father's arrival in Melbourne, my mother and their five children followed him to Australia. When my mother embarked, others complained that they would have a job to look after her five children. As it happened, however, everyone else was seasick and my mother tended to them! On the boat, Judah, the second oldest child, would sit up the front with his legs dangling over the side, watching the boat cutting through the water, so my mother always knew where to find him when he went missing. She made friends with an Italian woman on board and, as neither she nor my mother had a language in common, they communicated in sign language. This woman rolled her sleeves up and helped my mother to look after the children. Mother said she was an angel sent from heaven!

Not long before my mother and the children arrived in Australia, the Victorian Government had decided to irrigate land in the Shepparton area in order to replace the large squatters' estates with intensively cultivated farming. At the same time, members of the Melbourne Jewish community established the Shepparton Jewish Agricultural Settlement Fund to assist Jewish immigrants to find employment by settling on the land. They were assisted by a bequest left by Joseph Kronheimer, a local philanthropist. As a result of these initiatives by the state government and the Jewish community, my father and two other Jewish people he knew went to Shepparton to look at the irrigation system that was in the process of being established.

Although the three men were interested, my father wanted the small grant being offered to be split between eight families rather than three. His reasoning was that a *minyan* was needed in Shepparton so that the families could continue to observe the orthodox Jewish traditions. With eight men and two of their male children who had had their *bar mitzvah* (signifying adulthood in Jewish law), they would have a *minyan*. The other two men, who were less observant than my father, argued that to split the money among so many families would mean that no one would have enough. However, my father was adamant he would not be part of it without a *minyan* and eventually his view prevailed.

My father came to Shepparton with the intention of growing fruit, bought forty acres (sixteen hectares) of land and planted his first fruit trees. His land was five or six kilometres from the Shepparton township. When he first arrived, he lived in a tent and used wooden boxes for furniture. Life was tough and those first settlers had to contend with the floods which washed out the area. Later, my father built a shed to replace the tent.

As a practising orthodox Jew, my father followed the laws of the *Torah* in the way he cultivated the land. Although the orchards would take several years to become established, my father was guided by Jewish law which prevents the harvesting of fruit until the fourth year.

Until their trees bore fruit, most of the other Jewish orchardists had to work at other orchards at Ardmona, about ten or twelve kilometres away, which meant spending weekdays away from their families. My father was lucky to find work with Mr West, a local orchardist who also managed the Shepparton butter factory. As Mr West was very happy with his work, he kept him on, so my father was able to come home every evening to tend his own orchards.

When my mother and her five children joined my father in 1913, they lived in the shed my father had built. With subsidies from the government and the Jewish benefactor, however, my father was able to build a three-room weatherboard house. The house had a kitchen, dining room and bedroom, but as the years went by, verandas were added around the house and these were partitioned off to form bedrooms for the children. Although my parents originally had the bedroom inside the house, it had no ventilation and was very hot in summer, so they also moved to one of the bedrooms on the veranda.

My brother Dave was born in Shepparton in 1914, followed by Sarah, Freda, myself and Sam. I was born in 1921 and Sam in 1924. When Freda was born, my mother told the nurse to go and have another look as she had always had a boy, girl, boy, girl! Incidentally, Freda, whose Hebrew name was Shulamit, was given the second name Peace, as she was born on 11 November at 11.00 am. As well as her ten surviving children, my mother also gave birth to three children in Palestine who died in infancy. She never talked about them.

My father planted lucerne in his first year on the land and a wealthy pastoralist from Euroa bought the first crop to use as feed for his sheep. This provided my father with the funds to plant more fruit trees and buy dairy cattle to supply milk to the butter factory in Shepparton. My parents also established a vegetable garden, planting tomatoes, marrows, peas, carrots and whatever else was in season. The work was very strenuous and they had to scrape for every last penny.

With the cows came the question of milking on *Shabbos* and *Yom Tov*. Mr Davis, the neighbour across the road, saw that my father was an authentic man and said, 'Morry, I'll do your cows for you on Saturday.' Time went by and when *Yom Tov* came around and the other Jewish settlers didn't want to work, they asked Mr Davis if he would do their milking too. He replied, 'You do it on Saturday. Mo doesn't do it on Saturday, but you do, so you can do it your bloody selves!'

My father initially planted pear and peach trees, planting more every year. In his first years, the SPC (Shepparton Preserving Company) cannery advised local orchardists to grow a special kind of peach. This fruit, however, turned out to be unsuitable for canning as it fell to pieces. When the growers brought the fruit to the cannery, they were paid for it, but had to dump it at the tip. My mother decided this was not a good idea, so she scrubbed the floor boards on the sunny western side of the veranda, cut the peaches in half and laid them out to dry. The dried peaches were then sold to buy extra food for the family.

As well as the vegetables and fruit my family grew, my mother made dairy products. We also had some chickens, which my father killed, as he was a qualified *shochet*. Kosher beef had to come from Melbourne, but more often than not, it was spoilt in the hot weather by the time it arrived. Some years later, my father wrote to Rav Kook (of blessed memory) in Israel to explain the situation and ask for a young rabbi. He wanted this person not only to act as a *shochet*, but also be the *mohel*, the *melamud* and a general help to the community. In response to my father's request, Rabbi Yoffee arrived in Shepparton in 1923, to be followed a year later by his wife and children. (In later years Rabbi Yoffee was *shochet* and *Bal Kera* for Elwood Synagogue.)

The community originally conducted services in the house of Mr Cyprus, but when a piece of land with a small house on it became available up the road from our property, the community bought it to establish a synagogue. The synagogue was funded by the local community, with the help of the Shepparton Jewish Agricultural Settlement Fund in Melbourne.

Moshe and Leah Feiglin

Growing up on the orchard

I arrived on the orchard on 5 June 1921, the day in the Hebrew calendar known today as *Yom Yerushalayim* (Jerusalem Day). I am told that the doctor arrived soon after my birth to be welcomed by my howling. So began a life full of mostly joy and fruitfulness.

As the second youngest of our very large family, I was spoilt by my mother, as was my younger brother, Sam. Before our arrival, Mother had no time to do anything but what was essential to keep body and soul together for the family and home. By the time we came along, her life was easier so she vowed to spoil us, a mission the older members of my family would tell us was wonderfully well accomplished!

Our kitchen with its wood stove was the centre of our lives. Until electricity came to the area in 1936 this stove was our only form of heating. There was a servery between the kitchen and the dining room so the food could be passed through, but we ate most of our meals in the kitchen. It was also the place where we would sit and talk.

Food was stored in a box frame with shelves, with hessian bags hung over it. Water above the shelves dripped slowly down, wetting the hessian and keeping the food cool. Later we had an ice chest and ice was delivered from the butter factory in Shepparton once a week. When electricity was connected my mother bought her first refrigerator. Her choices were a Westinghouse or a Frigidaire, and she did her market research very thoroughly. After much thought, she finally decided on the Westinghouse and even though this fridge would be tiny by today's standards, it made a huge difference to her life.

Eventually we had a washhouse and bathroom near the house, but when I was very young, my mother did the washing in the canal alongside the house. That canal provided our house with running water, pumped by a windmill into an elevated tank above the house, which gravitated the water into the kitchen, bathroom and washhouse. At first our hot water was heated in the copper and had to be brought in from the washhouse, but later we had pipes running through the stove in the kitchen which provided hot water.

The dining room was only used for dinner on Friday night, Saturday lunch and *Yom Tov*, although in winter the family would have *Shabbos* dinner in the kitchen where it was warm. It was only when electricity was connected that we had radiators in the other rooms. Until then our lighting was provided by kerosene lamps.

* * *

When my mother was pregnant with me, she had diphtheria and was told she would not be able to nurse me. My father bought a young heifer (female calf), which not only provided milk for me, but also became a house pet. Her name was Doreen. She would feed along the road and if you rattled a bucket, she would come and stand in position to be milked. She not only supplied milk for us, but for the neighbours as well, and when I was old enough I milked her too.

I have no recollection of the first twenty-two months of

my life; however, my first recollection was of crawling up the ramp that lead to the house (I did not walk till I was over two years old). Rabbi Yoffee, who was staying with us at the time, was walking behind me, pushing me on my behind with his tan shoes, laughing out loud. I still remember this!

One day, before I could walk, it so happened that one of the workers had stopped the lorry with its two horses near the house. I crawled out and sat myself under the lorry, unbeknown to the driver, who came bounding out of the house, jumped up to his seat and did a U turn. This I remember very clearly. I decided to crawl out of danger and I recall the lorry's iron wheels scraping my stomach as I crawled as hard as I could. Where to crawl? Well, my angel was there, guiding me in the right direction. The driver happened to look back, saw me, stopped the horses and ran back, calling to my father. My father rushed out, picked me up and sat me on a small patch of grass. To see if I was hurt, he gave me a fence strainer (machine used to tighten fence wires) while he and my mother watched to see that I had all my faculties. That was but the first time my guardian angel watched over me.

The years that followed are not clear to me, although certain little facts do come back. One of my clear memories is of the trike (tricycle) I had when I was around four years old. For some reason it was never oiled, so it used to squeak, squeaking its way to a worn-out wreck.

In the yard around the house, we had chickens that we regarded as part of the family – pets which would come up and feed from your hand. I do not know how we came by the few bantams we had, which were picturesque little birds, especially the rooster with its beautifully coloured feathers. I planned to catch one of the bantams and put it under a box. My aim was for it to lay eggs and have chickens, but it just happened that I caught the rooster. At that stage nobody had enlightened me about 'the birds and the bees'. I left the rooster under the box and promptly forgot about him. I recall my mother looking for him, wondering what could have happened. Ultimately his skeleton was found and I confessed, explaining why I had placed him there.

We always had one cow as a house cow, so we had milk in the house, and mother also used to make cheese and butter. When you have a cow, you cannot milk it for the three months before she calves, so for that time we had no homemade cheese and butter and had to rely on the factory in Shepparton. Missing our homemade dairy products, I would come home from school and walk around the paddock to see if the cow had calved.

One day I found the newly-born calf, which the mother had instinctively hidden in the paddock behind a clod of earth to protect it from wild beasts. I lifted up its leg and saw four teats, thinking that it was wonderful we had another heifer, as it would mean we would have another cow. I came back to the house to tell my brothers that the cow had calved and her heifer was up in the paddock. They waited a few hours until the calf could walk and brought both the cow and calf back to the warmth of the shed. They asked me how I knew it was a heifer and I said, 'I lifted its leg and saw that it had four teats.' To this my brother replied, 'Well, haven't you got two?' It was a bull calf!

One day, my mother was doing some baking and needed a lemon, so I saw the opportunity to go to the Beresinskys up the road as they had a lemon tree. I was five and they had a daughter almost my age, so I took a billy and off I went. I stayed there until Mrs Beresinsky suggested it was late and I should go home.

I was notorious for always playing near the canal, dangling my feet in the water. As it was already late and I was not to be found anywhere, my parents thought I must have fallen into the channel and drowned. I came back from the Beresinskys to see my parents wading through the water looking for me. When I saw them, I said in my childish Yiddish, '*Voshi* (instead of *vos ist*, meaning what is it)? My mother climbed out of the channel as quickly as she could, soaking wet, and gave me a great big hug, relieved that I had come to no harm.

This reminds me of the hug Richard Pratt received from his mother several years later. It happened when I went with my father to visit the Pratts, who were looking to go into business with some friends of theirs. Richard, then aged about four, was at home with his cousin, Max Opfall – and his parents were out. While we were waiting for the Pratts to return, we walked around the yard looking for something to do. Max, to show us how strong he was, sank an axe into a log and picked up the log, axe and all. After a while, we went out to the road to see if the Pratts were coming and, as we waited on the side of the road, a car approached. In it were the Pratts and Opfalls. They pulled up on the opposite side of the road and, as soon as Richard saw his mother getting out of the car, he ran across the road towards her. He did not notice the approaching car, but I did and raced up, pulling Richard off the road. The car swerved around us, but we had a lucky escape. Richard was unscathed, but Mrs Pratt's hug showed how aware she was of the danger that had passed.

Incidentally, my brother Judah cured me of playing too near the water. One day I was sitting on a small bridge over an irrigation channel. Judah snuck up behind me, grabbed me by the shirt and braces and plunged me into the water, keeping me under for long enough to frighten the life out of me. I didn't go near the water on my own for about three years after that, but when the older ones went swimming, I would go with them. When they tried to coax me into the water, I would be reluctant to go, screaming, 'But you'll dunk me!'

My brother Abraham had gone back to Israel as a single man to look after our grandparents. Whilst there, he married and had two children, returning to Shepparton with his family when I was five or six years old. They lived in a house near ours and Abraham worked in the orchard. One day I was watching Abraham pruning a tree when he asked me to go on an errand for him. In my arrogance I said, 'Who the hell are you to tell me what to do?' 'What do you mean?' he replied. 'I'm your eldest brother!' I ran as fast as I could into the house to ask my mother if this was true!

In 1926 my father bought his first car, a Chrysler tourer. I was so excited that, even though there was a heavy frost, I went outside the next morning in my pyjamas, with bare feet. I just had to see the car and sit behind the steering wheel to have an imaginary ride.

By the way, the car always seemed to have petrol blockages and it was a common sight to see my father at the side of the road with the bonnet raised, pumping air from the car's vacuum tank to the petrol tank. Sedans were coming on to the market and my father decided he wanted his tourer converted to a sedan by installing wind-up windows. He took it to Mr

McNeil, a blacksmith and wheelwright and a very capable tradesman. When Mr McNeil removed the seats, he examined the pipe which brought the petrol from the petrol tank to the vacuum tank under the bonnet and then to the carburetors. Looking carefully, he noticed that this pipe had been flattened, restricting the petrol flow. Not only did we end up with a sedan, but that was also the end of the petrol blockages.

In 1926 my brother Mark was at high school and had been playing with a big, heavy ball used for shot put. The ball apparently fell out of his hand and landed on his shoulder. A few days later he developed a high temperature and my father took him to Mooroopna Hospital to see Dr Florence, a woman doctor (not common at that time, especially in rural areas). I went with them in a horse-drawn jinker, and how well I still recall it. When we arrived at the hospital, my father tied the horse to the tree, left me sitting in the gig and walked with Mark up to the doctor's rooms. They were away for a considerable time and my father and the doctor finally appeared on the veranda without Mark. There they stood talking to each other for some time. To me it seemed an eternity.

Finally, my father came towards me and I could see by his walk that he was extremely upset. He untied the horse and got into the jinker. My brother's Yiddish name was Modche, but in my childish, five-year-old Yiddish, I asked, 'Voo is Moshke (where is Moshke)?' And he answered, 'Mark is not coming home with us.' He had been diagnosed with blood poisoning, which in those days before penicillin was lethal. I remember the sadness in the house. Just a few days later, Mark was gone. I can recall his body being placed in the tray of a 1924 Chev (Chevrolet) truck to be taken to Fawkner Cemetery in Melbourne. I also remember following the truck for some way up the road as it drove off. I presume my father went with the body.

Around 1927, word got around the Jewish community in Shepparton that the film *The Jazz Singer* was going to be screened at the Lyric Theatre. It was very exciting for me, as I had never seen a film before. Equally momentous was the fact that my mother decided to go too, accompanied by those of us who were still living at home. It was not as simple as going to the bus stop and catching a bus! Rather, the old spring cart used for carrying the fruit out of the orchard was to take us.

Mother arranged for one of our employees, a Hungarian Jewish man who had been a light horseman in the Hungarian Army during World War I, to be our coachman. Even though we had two faster horses, Mother was adamant that old Prince would be the one to take us. Our coachman protested, but Mother insisted, so we all tumbled into the cart and set off at the grand old speed of around three kilometres an hour. Needless to say, we were not booked for speeding! Finally arriving in Shepparton with no booking, we ended up in the front row of the theatre, very close to the screen.

The film was silent and black and white, with captions explaining the major scenes. From my front row seat, I could look down into the orchestra pit while Al Jolson, the cantor, was singing on the screen above me. Music came from the phonograph, which had to be wound up to play, and the record was synchronized with the singing of the actor.

The film finished in time for us to hop into our Rolls Royce, with good old Prince as the motor. We were all tired by then and it seemed to take forever to get home. Our coachman was not at all happy as the outing had lasted an eternity, but at least we had plenty to talk about for some time. It was a truly memorable experience for a six-year-old and one I can still remember today – over eight and a half decades later!

Often on Saturday nights, when the days were long enough, our outing of the week was to go into Shepparton, where the shops were open until nine o'clock. We would go shopping and collect the mail from the post office. My father bought his Pontiac in 1936 and I recall as many of us as the car would hold piling into it and setting off. One evening Mother did not go as she wanted to clean her new refrigerator. She carefully took everything out of it and as the globe was loose, it came out too. She then went about her job with a wet cloth. The cloth must have come into contact with the globe socket and Mother was thrown backwards on to the floor. We came back from our outing to find her sitting in an armchair sobbing, a common consequence of electric shock. This was not a very pleasant way for her to learn about the dangers of electricity!

The Feiglins, Shepparton, 1928
with Aaron 3rd from the right in 2nd row

I couldn't have chosen better parents

It is said that one cannot choose one's parents and so I have to accept this. If I had had a choice, however, I could not have wished for better.

My mother was a genius, one of the wisest, kindest and most industrious women you could ever meet. I have already told the story of how she rescued the first crop of peaches destined for the tip to dry out and sell. This, however, was not an isolated example and she showed such ingenuity throughout her life. There was nothing she would not tackle. She did all the cooking and cleaning, washing, ironing and sewing, with none of the labour-saving devices we have today. Although my older brothers and sisters left for Melbourne when they had finished their schooling in Shepparton, she still had five children at home as I was growing up. By that stage, my parents were more established and my mother had a few hours help once a week, but she was always busy and hardly had a moment to herself.

She would make *lokshen* by mixing and kneading the ingredients, rolling the dough out thinly, then rolling it up, chopping it into strips, gently shaking it until the strips separated and leaving it on the bed to dry. She made her own cheese and was a fantastic baker, whipping up sponge cakes, strudel, cheesecake and *eier kichel*, all without an electric mixer or any other sophisticated equipment. Instead she had a large three-pronged fork with a wooden handle which she would use to beat the egg whites until they were stiff, adding them to her delicious sponge cakes. Her *eier kichel* were famous and those produced for my *bar mitzvah* were made to perfection.

Sometimes Mother would bake *challahs* for Friday night, although my father had arranged with the bakery to make French bread with just flour, yeast and water and to bake it on the hot pod of the oven, making it kosher. The bread was delivered by horse and cart twice a week and my mother stored it in a large milk can.

Shabbos was a special time for our family. On Friday nights we would usually have chicken soup and chicken; and even today, when we sing *zmires* on a Friday night, I can smell my mother's chicken soup! We always had compote made from fruit from the orchard, as well as prunes and other dried fruit. On Saturdays, we would come home from *shul* and make *kiddush*, followed by cakes and *kugel*. My father would then conduct more Jewish learning, after which we would have lunch. Usually my mother would make *cholent* and rice, which used to put me to sleep as it was very heavy!

Each *Yom Tov* was special and my mother would cook the traditional foods for each festival. For *Pesach* our place would be turned upside down; the whole house was cleaned, the usual dishes put away and the special *Pesach* dishes taken down from the cupboards where they were stored for the rest of the year. It was a huge amount of work, not just for my mother but for my father and all the children as well. In my later years, we were fortunate to be able to build our house in East St Kilda and I made sure we had a special *Pesach* kitchen so we could be saved all that effort.

Mother never used a recipe, learning from her mother in Palestine and later working things out for herself. It was just a pity that no one thought of writing down her recipes!

The washing was done in a big washhouse. There was a copper to heat up the water, with a wood fire underneath it which had to be stoked. Mother would boil up the washing, then rinse it and hang it out on lines in the yard. As she never wasted anything, she would even save the fat from the meat she cooked to boil up and make her own soap.

Mother had a sewing machine and would make all the bed linen. She made all the boys' shirts as well as the girls' dresses. One day the teacher called Sam and me out to the platform in front of the class to point out our shirts – which we called *bluskes*. 'Class,' he said, 'I want you have a look at these children and go home and tell your mothers how they are dressed. They are always clean and tidy. Your mothers should follow their example.' My mother would make our *bluskes* of heavy blue material for winter and lighter blue cotton for summer. She would buy bolts of material from Fairley's General Store in Shepparton (some of which I still have, over seventy years later). She would go into Shepparton in a horse and gig and the image of bolts of material being loaded on to the gig is still very clear to me.

Mother brought a hand-operated sewing machine with her from Palestine. Later she became quite 'modern', buying a Singer treadle sewing machine. This made her life a lot easier. She was always busy sewing and mending and, as far as my parents could afford it, we children would have new clothes for *Yom Tov* .

Saturday morning was the only time Mother rested, staying

in bed until late. She was the only member of our family who did not go to *shul* and Sam and I vied for the privilege of taking her a cup of tea in bed before we left. *Rosh Hashannah* and *Yom Kippur* were the only days Mother attended services.

As well as running the household and looking after our physical needs, my mother was always there to look after our emotional needs. When we were naughty she would never smack us, although my father would occasionally scold us and I would have to kiss his hand and apologise. Mother, however, would express her disapproval through sarcasm. For example, if Sam and I wanted to go fishing, she would say, 'Sure, go fishing!' This was a clear message that she didn't want us to go, but we chose to take her words literally, which gave us the excuse to disobey.

I had great rapport with her and she was the first person to whom I would turn to discuss any problems or to ask for advice. When I was at primary school, Mother had diphtheria and was in hospital for over two weeks. Finally, when the day arrived for her to come home, I could not contain myself and asked the headmaster if I could go home early in the afternoon. He only gave me permission after asking many questions, as he did not seem to understand the longing I had to be with my mother again.

In 1940, when I was nineteen, the army was conscripting young men to fight in the war and I received my call-up papers, instructing me to report for a medical examination. I had a very heavy heart and, on the Saturday before, I took my mother a cup of tea and sat with her for a long time, discussing my fate. By the time I arrived at the synagogue, the service was almost over and my father reprimanded me later. 'What's the big idea of coming to the service when it's nearly finished?' he said. Mother then said, 'Moishe, sometimes it's necessary to come late.' Not another word was said, as my father realised that it must have been serious. As it turned out, although I passed the medical, I was exempted from the army on the grounds that our orchard was supplying food for the army, an activity deemed critical to the war effort.

My mother's kindness extended beyond her beloved family. In 1903, when she had just given birth to my brother Judah, one of her neighbours, Chana Mushin, had also given birth to a son, Maccabee. Mrs Mushin became very ill with diphtheria and was unable to feed her son, so my mother took him in and nurtured him until such time as Mrs Mushin was able to resume looking after her son. Today, Maccabee's daughter, Ruth, is helping me to write my story, something which may not have been possible without my mother's help!

Some year later in Shepparton, when a woman who was six months pregnant realised that her baby was coming, she asked that Mother be told. My mother immediately contacted her sister-in-law to come as well, and rode, side-saddle, to look after the pregnant woman. They delivered the baby, but the mother was in great danger, bleeding profusely. According to Jewish law, the mother's life must come before the baby's so my mother and her sister-in-law put the baby to one side to tend to the mother. When they managed to stem the bleeding and knew that she would live, they turned to the baby girl and saw that she was still breathing.

The two women cleaned the baby and managed to feed her with an eyedropper. They then found a shoebox, wrapped up the baby and took mother and baby by horse and cart to hospital. After spending some time in hospital, mother and baby were ready to go home, but the matron thought the baby had little chance of survival. It was a miracle that she did, and she developed normally, with no visible signs of the difficulties she had had at birth. Her parents named her Tikvah, the Hebrew word for hope. She is now a great-grandmother living in East St Kilda.

During the war, there was a shortage of labour and the rookies (air force pilots in training) based in Shepparton would pick fruit in our orchards during the two-and-a-half hours they had off duty in the afternoon. My mother always fed them the best of everything and when I asked her why she was going to so much trouble for them, she replied, 'Aaron, you should know that they are children who have mothers. They are going off to war and one must have feeling for every human being, especially considering where they are going.'

My father was a man of great integrity and intelligence and a very energetic and hard-working person. He would get up before daybreak, say his prayers and devote time to his Jewish studies before going off to work. As I was growing up, the family had begun making boxes for the orchardists in the area and we had employees who worked in the orchards, so he was able to cut back on physical work.

Although I didn't see my father during the day, we always went to *shul* together on Saturday morning and he played an important role in our Jewish education. Although we had a *melamed* who would come to our home each week, my father would spend time with us at night, and especially approaching my *bar mitzvah*; he taught me my *maftir*, gave me *tefillin* and taught me how to *daven*. He also helped other boys in the community to prepare for their *bar mitzvahs*.

Unfortunately I was no more interested in my Jewish studies than my secular studies, but my father would say, 'One day you will be glad of learning what you've learnt.' And that day finally came!

I have already told the story about my father leading services in Port Said on his way to Australia. He continued to lead services in Shepparton with his sweet tenor voice and sensitivity; his *Megillah* reading was like a piece of music. I did not leave Shepparton until I was seventeen years old and to hear my father *daven* was all I knew. It was only as I grew older and spent more time away from home that I began to see how beautifully he prayed.

To grow up to be orthodox Jews was normal for us children as our parents were such wonderful role models. My father's concern about ensuring his children maintained the orthodox Jewish traditions, however, extended beyond observing the traditions and having a Jewish education. He did not object to our non-Jewish friends, but he also wanted to make sure we didn't become too involved with them. Tennis was a popular game when we were at high school, so my father built a tennis court on our property. Our friends – both Jewish and non-Jewish – would come over after school and on Sundays and my father was able to keep an eye on us while we were having a good time playing tennis!

My father's word was known to be as good as a written contract. In his early days in Shepparton when he was working for Mr West, Mr West's manager asked Father to estimate the amount of fruit on the trees. He came up with a figure, but when the fruit was harvested, they were one box short of his estimate. As a man of his word, he went out into the orchard and found some fruit that had been missed until he had made up the extra box. This could not help but impress his employers.

As my father was a man of habit, he would go into Shepparton to collect his mail at the same time each morning. Years later, the local barrister and solicitor told my brother that if he had a difficult problem, he would make a point of bumping into my father as he was clearing his post office box so that he could casually have a discussion with him. He knew that, more often than not, Father would give him an alternative point of view to his own, which would be very useful.

One day I was at the cannery in Shepparton when a man came up to me and asked if I was a Feiglin. He told me he had been buying boxes from my father, but he went broke and could not afford to pay for them. Father came out to his property to take his order, coming very close and grabbing his lapel as he spoke, which was a habit of his. This man confessed that he had no money to pay his previous bill, to which my father replied, 'I didn't come here to collect your money, but to collect next year's order. I know you'll pay me when you can.' Many years later the man still had not paid, but he had not forgotten my father's kindness.

My father played a very important role in the lives of the Jewish internees at Tatura. These boys, who had fled to Britain to escape Nazi persecution in Europe before the outbreak of war in 1939, became enemy aliens when war was declared. They were interned by the British, but as Britain had interned so many refugees, she asked other Commonwealth countries to help out. So, in mid-1940, over two and a half thousand were sent to Australia on the *Dunera*. These refugees became known as the 'Dunera boys'. After a difficult voyage, during which they were treated brutally by the British guards, they were regarded with great suspicion by the Australian authorities, who feared they might be spies for the Nazis! Some were interned in Hay in New South Wales, but were later moved to Tatura in Victoria, where the climate was less harsh and more suitable for a camp. After the war, some of these men returned to Britain.

Tatura was only fifteen kilometres from Shepparton and, as soon as my father heard about these 'enemy aliens', he obtained permission to enter the camp. He was mainly interested in the orthodox Jewish boys and he arranged to supply them with kosher food and books. He would spend time with them and they looked forward to his company. Soon the major in charge of the camp allowed him to have free access to the internees, the only civilian to be granted this privilege. In 1942, when the internees were allowed to leave the camp and help with the war effort, my father employed several of them to work in the orchards.

Father was a hard-working and energetic man, but he gave us quite a scare in 1937. He was driving through an intersection on the main road when a young driver approached at high speed along the cross road, testing to see how fast his Ford would go. The traffic was nowhere near as heavy as it is today and he reckoned it was a reasonable risk to cross the main road. Unfortunately he was wrong and he slammed into Father's new Pontiac.

Our phone rang and I picked it up to hear that Father had had an accident and had been taken to the local hospital. Needless to say, my mother was devastated, as we all were. My father had a fractured skull, but managed to pull through and eventually returned to his normal self.

My parents had a very harmonious relationship. They would have their important discussions in their bedroom and although we could hear their voices, there was never an argument. Father discussed everything with Mother and would always take her advice. His view was that you should always 'have a go' and he would say in Hebrew, 'You will be blessed with everything you do, but if you don't do, how can you be blessed?' Mother, however, was more cautious and held him back in making business decisions. He probably could have made a lot more money if he hadn't always taken her advice!

Moshe Feiglin, Melbourne, 1952

Four

Off to Orrvale State School

When I was of school age, I lined up with my older brothers and sisters and off I marched, the three kilometres to Orrvale State School.

One of my first teachers was Miss 'Bottles' Bartelles, who produced very nice drawings with captions written beneath them, which she would read to us. One day, she asked me to come out to the platform at the front of the class to test my memory. I ran up and rattled off 'Hey diddle diddle, the cat and the fiddle, the cow jumped over the moon. The little dog laughed to see such fun and the dish ran away with the spoon.' I recall saying it at such speed that she was left speechless for a few minutes, but I think she was impressed.

Snakes sometimes provided a diversion in the classroom. Although they hibernate in winter, in summer they were a constant danger and we always had to be on the lookout for them. One day a snake came into our classroom. The headmaster told us to step up onto our seats and keep still. He then made a noise behind the snake to get it to move, and once it crawled out to the veranda, he killed it by breaking its back with a stick. Another day we were sitting in the shade under a tree in the playground when a walloping big brown snake crawled passed us. Our teacher happened to be there with a shovel, which he gave me. As the snake was about to crawl under the school building, I tried to hit it, but was not quick enough. The snake disappeared and we were lucky it didn't bother us again.

Aside from little dramas like this, school was fairly routine. As the year rolled on, I looked forward to the end of the year, marked by the first Christmas carols. Why so? Simply because within a few weeks, we would break up and the long summer holidays would be with us.

The years went by and, when I reached the ripe old age of eleven, Mr Rumpff, who was both headmaster and class teacher and incidentally lived on till one hundred and three, gave each of us a small plot of land to plant whatever we wished. Gardening day was once a week and even though it was good to get out of the classroom, it was not without its dangers. Before tending our plots, we would all rush to the tool room to get our preferred tools. One day I rushed out of the tool room with a fork in my hands, its prongs facing outwards in front of me. Just at that moment, my best friend, Jack Pottinger, came running towards me and I almost speared him. Fortunately, I saw the danger and had the presence of mind to drop the fork and we finished up in each other's arms.

In trying to decide what to grow, my friend Ted Baker and I studied the vegetable book and came up with the idea of growing horseradish. We liked the sound of it because it was something new, but neither of us had any idea what it was or what to do with it. Anyhow, we tended these plants and they grew tall, but still nobody could tell us what to do with them. Eventually they were dug up and destroyed, but it was a shame I relied on that book rather than consulting my mother. Had somebody said 'chrein' she would have known immediately!

The plot of soil where we grew the horseradish happened to be alongside Mr Rumpff's house, next to a plot of strawberries he was growing. The strawberries grew and Mr Rumpff eagerly kept watch over one that was almost ripe. One day I was standing looking at our horseradish when he came up to look at his strawberry. It was gone and, as I was standing there, he thought I must have taken it! Maybe I did but I do not recall it. Seeing me there and the strawberry gone, he immediately dug his hand into his right pocket. I knew what was in there – the strap! Since I was a good runner, I took off with him wielding the strap behind me. I think I broke the long-jump record as I escaped, leaping over the flowerbed towards the small gate, which luckily was open. I slammed the gate behind me, spoiling his run, and ran towards home. I was not exactly the teacher's pet and this incident definitely did not help our relationship.

Around that time, Mr Rumpff's son, a little fellow we knew as Sixpence, was a student at Shepparton High School and would come back to his home at Orrvale State School by bike. One rather cold day we were on our way home when one of the big larrikins suggested to the others they make a rope out of their overcoats, string it across the road and tip Sixpence off his bike. As the road was made out of rough pieces of blue metal, to fall on it would cause bad injuries.

The big kids waited and, in due course, Sixpence came riding along. On seeing the rope across the road, he put his head down and tail up and speeded up as much as he could, thinking he could break through the rope. This would not necessarily be so, because hitting the rope with his front wheel may have caused the back to lift, thus tipping him off.

I could see the danger and placed myself next to the ringleader, making out that I was there to help. However, as Sixpence approached and came very close, I stood back and shoved the ringleader forward. The rope fell from his hands and Sixpence rode by without incident. The next day, Mr Rumpff came up to me and thanked me profusely. This marked a definite thaw in our previously cool relationship. By the way, the older, bigger boys often liked to push us younger ones around and we would get into fights. I was often involved and even though I had plenty of blood noses, I gave plenty back to my opponents!

During the summer months our class would head down to the irrigation channel where the level of the water was deep enough for swimming. Before leaving we would undress and put on our swimming gear in the shelter sheds. One day my friend Jack, seeing my *tzitzis*, asked, 'Is this to keep the flies off your doodle?' In the summer months, when flies were plentiful, they tried to get into the horses' eyes, looking for moisture. As a result, we would attach five chords to the horses' winkers (head gear) and by shaking their heads, the horses could drive the flies away. The logic of Jack's question was admirable, but I was happy to enlighten him about their real significance! Incidentally, Jack and I were the best of friends until, sadly, he passed away in September 2005.

One particular day it was blowing a stiff southerly and was very cold, so we could not go swimming. Instead, we were given practical hints on lifesaving in the classroom. Mr Rumpff explained that if you got into difficulty under water and you could not surface, you should cup your hands and put them above your head and kick your legs and this would bring you to the surface. So, on a very hot day, I went for a swim in the channel out in front of our house. It was one-and-a-half metres deep. I was in the water by myself, doing all sorts of trick somersaults and standing on my hands, but when I tried to surface, I kept scraping along the bottom of the channel. I panicked and the harder I tried to surface, the longer I remained on the bottom of the channel. Suddenly, my guardian angel whispered in my ear, 'What did Rumpffy say?' I did what he said and immediately surfaced, with only a few seconds to spare!

Orrvale Primary School, 1928, with Principal, Mr Rumpff (back row right) and Aaron in back row of students, fifth from right

Our farmyard animals

In introducing this story of mine, I mentioned that I grew up surrounded by all sorts of animals. We always had dogs as pets and, as you will see from some of the incidents I will relate, they played an important part in my life.

Our lives were not easy when I was a young child and diphtheria, a terrible infection of the throat, made things more difficult to bear. It is a highly dangerous and infectious disease and although none of the males in our family were smitten with it, all the females had several bouts. If you contracted it, you were isolated in the infectious diseases ward in Mooroopna Hospital and not until the infection had completely cleared up were you allowed to go home.

I was not more than five years old, but I faintly recall my oldest sister, Bertha, having diphtheria. At that time we had a dog called Tip, whose name came about because he was completely black, except for a white tip on his tail. He was very attached to Bertha and when she went to hospital in a two-wheeled gig, Tip followed. When she was admitted, Tip silently followed her into her room and settled under her bed. The nurses took a liking to him, saw that he had food and water and left the door open for him to go outside. He would go outside, relieve himself and back he would come to settle under Bertha's bed again. Hospital hygiene standards would not permit that sort of thing today, but what a comfort Tip was to Bertha at that time.

Tip was just as protective of the whole family. Around this time, another Jewish family, the Dabscheks, purchased two orchards, one to the north and the other to the south of ours. Sarah Dabschek was being courted by Mr Pushett (whom she later married) and one Friday night, the couple was walking past our house towards the Dabscheks' house at the end of the lane. Tip made a heck of a noise, not letting them pass, so they called out for help. I got out of bed and called Tip to come – otherwise they would have found it difficult to get home!

When I was nine or ten, we got another puppy, a Queensland heeler/collie cross we called Sailor. He had short black and white hair and needed very little training as he was good at working things out for himself.

We had a neighbour, a girl of my age, who would often come to visit and would tease Sailor while he was in his kennel. Sailor didn't like that and put a stop to it by making a big fuss as soon as she touched the kennel. It sounded as if he was going to eat her and she soon stopped annoying him.

Sailor used to follow one of our young employees into the orchard and keep himself busy by catching mice. The lad's job was to pick up the cuttings left on the ground after the trees had been pruned and burn them. To do this he lit a fire in a tub drawn along by a horse. Although the horse was a good distance ahead, the fire would sometimes erupt suddenly as the lad threw the cuttings into the tub, heating up the horse's rump. A long length of rope was tied to the horse and the lad would tug at it if the horse failed to stop on his command. One day the fire must have been a little warmer than usual and the horse took off. The lad did not manage to catch the rope in time to stop the horse, so Sailor ran forward, took the rope in his mouth and pulled on it until the horse stopped.

Three of my siblings – Judah, Joe and Bertha – all married in the same year in Melbourne and each time my parents went to the wedding. The first time they went by car, but the second and third times they decided to go by train. The first time they went to the station, Sailor followed them and when they got on the train, he went home. However, the second time they went by train Sailor was not satisfied, so he lay down on the train tracks and would not move. The station master came along, picked him up, moved him to a sheltered position, covered him and fed him. There he stayed for the five or six days until my parents returned and when they got off the train, he went home happily with them.

Sailor decided to follow us to school one day. My sister and I rode our bikes and he turned up while we were having assembly in the main hall. The headmistress was conducting the assembly from the platform when Sailor came in, went up to the platform and stood with his paws up on the platform, looking around for us. The headmistress asked, 'Who owns this cur?' I owned up, so she asked me to remove him.

I put Sailor near the back fence and didn't see him again until lunchtime, when the deputy headmaster was walking around, surrounded by a dozen students, asking if a black and white dog belonged to anyone. Realising it was Sailor, I owned up to the teacher. Sailor had found my bike amongst hundreds of others and would not let anyone go near the twelve bikes surrounding mine which belonged to students who wanted to go home for lunch.

Sailor was protective of all our possessions, whether animate or inanimate. Father had a turkey which he would feed every morning but one morning, the turkey flew over his head, then ran out the gate and up the road. Father began chasing the turkey and as he ran past my bedroom window, he called out to me to help him. I got out of bed, ran out of the house with bare feet, hopped on my bike and chased the turkey up the road, with Sailor in hot pursuit. The turkey ran in to a ploughed field where I was unable to ride my bike and it was difficult to run barefoot. Sizing up the situation, Sailor chased the turkey and when he caught up to him, put his head over the turkey's neck, pressed the turkey to his chest and held him. It would have been normal for a dog to grab the turkey by the neck, but Sailor somehow instinctively understood that this was not acceptable. He may not have understood the Jewish laws of ritual slaughter, but he seemed to know that my father was the only one who killed animals.

Not long after that, a woman came to our house with some chickens for my father to kill. She talked to my mother while my father was dealing with the chickens and when he was finished, she came outside to collect them. Suddenly I heard screaming and ran outside to find the dog preventing the woman from touching the chickens. He had pulled her to the ground and just would not let her go, acting as if he thought the chickens belonged to my father! Finally, we put the chickens in a bag and gave them to the woman who rode off on her bike. On her way home she stopped to visit another Jewish woman who lived down at the end of our road, which was a dead end. While she was inside, Sailor sat outside and waited, but when she came out of the house a half an hour later with her bag of chickens, Sailor once again pulled her to the ground. Again she started screaming, sitting on the road and prevented by Sailor from moving. It was only after my intervention that Sailor allowed her to get on her bike with the bag and ride away.

Another time, a man by the name of Mr Sneider came to Shepparton to buy an orchard. One winter's day, he came to our place with the estate agent. As it was warm, he left his coat out on the veranda while he went to look at an orchard. After a while he came back to get his coat, but the dog caught him and would not let him move, as he thought he was taking something of ours. Following that incident, Sailor would not let any of Mr Sneider's five children come on to our property, so if they came to visit we would have to tie him up.

Yet another time we had bought a new spray pump and some of the orchardists came to look at it. When one of them picked up the crank handle, Sailor growled at them, warning them that they could look but not touch. He was not at all unfriendly, but always looked after what he thought were our interests and he was such an intelligent dog that he sometimes seemed to think more like a person!

When I was around ten years old, we had another dog called Jack. I had been with my mother at a nearby property where she was helping another woman give birth to her child and Jack had come with us. As my mother was going to be there for some time, I was to return home with only Jack for company. Normally that would not have been a problem, but on the way I had to pass some gypsies camping in a paddock. As gypsies had a bad reputation, especially for stealing, I was petrified. I took a handkerchief out of my pocket, tied it to

Jack's collar and, holding on to it, let him guide me past. Without the sense of security he gave me, I would not have been able to keep going.

Jack also looked after me on the day of my *bar mitzvah*. After the synagogue service, my mother prepared a *kiddush* for the men and boys at our home. Afterwards, they went home and the women came to congratulate my parents and enjoy my mother's hospitality. It was a frosty day in June and after lunch I lay down on the lawn and fell asleep. My friend Jack Soafkin (of blessed memory) arrived with his mother, snuck up on me and got ready to give me a whack on my behind. As soon as he raised his arm, Jack grabbed him by the arm and I woke up.

Many years later, we had a kelpie dog called Shim, which also knew how to look after people. Angelo, our worker who lived in the cottage on our property, had a little daughter called Josie who would play in their garden. Josie liked to run out on to the road between the cottage and the shed and as this was where the forklift was working, she always had to be watched. One day, her mother, seeing she was in danger, called out to her, 'Josie, *vene quoi* (come here).' Shim instinctively sensed what was happening and ran out to Josie, shielding her body and gently edging her out of the way and back to her mother.

Our neighbour's large collie was also famous for rescuing a small child. The Bennetts had three daughters and a son, who was the youngest in the family. When this little boy was around two years old, he loved to crawl around outside. In those days the baker would deliver bread in his horse-drawn cart. One day, the little boy managed to crawl under the cart, between its four big wheels. The dog noticed the baker running up to the cart to start the two horses on their way, so it rushed up to the cart and, with full force, knocked the child out of the way. Without the dog's intervention, the little boy would almost certainly have been crushed by those big wheels.

Our cats may not have been as memorable as our dogs, but we always had them around the house and one of them had a nasty accident one day. We had a two-roomed washhouse adjoining the house where the washing was done and the poultry cleaned. The washhouse had a south-facing window and in hot weather, a cool southerly breeze was most pleasant. After cleaning the poultry, my mother would throw the unwanted bits out the window and the cat would be there to enjoy them. She would then throw the boiling water she had used for the cleaning out the window. One day, my mother did not notice the cat and threw out the water, scalding the poor animal on one side of her body. The cat lost all the hair on the burnt side and it eventually grew back grey. Before that she was only known as 'Katz' (the Yiddish word for cat), but from then on, she became known as the 'Grey-Black Cat'.

Earlier in my story, I wrote about my efforts to get the rooster to produce chickens, but I eventually found out about the 'birds and the bees'. As well as bantams, we had black and white fowls; these poultry interbred, resulting in a three-quarter-sized fowl. Bantams are wonderful mothers and ours would lay their eggs well-hidden and almost impossible to find. After three weeks the bantam mother would emerge with a cluster of chickens, usually around twelve or fourteen. The mother hen would move around with her chickens, scratching around looking for food, watched by the grey-black cat.

The cat had worked out that a chicken made a nice

breakfast, but after losing several chickens, the mother hen soon learnt to protect them. She made sure that they followed her and, if one moved out in front, she would grab it by the beak and fling it back over her shoulder. The mother hen also watched the cat and if it showed signs of approaching, she would fly straight into its face. Eventually the cat learnt to respect the hen!

Years later, after I was married, I decided to buy some fifty day-old chicks. Not far from our cottage I built a large shelter with a special globe to keep them warm. I made the cover out of strips of woollen material about forty centimetres long and the chickens could move in and out, keeping themselves at the right temperature.

My brother Joe came to stay for a weekend and parked his car near the chicken shelter. One chicken managed to get under the car and perched on the tail shaft so that when Joe got into the car and reversed, the chicken was not quick enough and lost its head. That meant I had only forty-nine chickens.

When the chickens were beginning to lay, I settled them into the chicken yard further away from the cottage. The next morning, when I went out to feed them, I noticed a hole under the wire netting around the yard and not one chicken inside. I went out into the orchard to look for them and soon found that they were able to run neither towards or away from me, as they lay dead amongst the fruit trees. It looked as if I had lost them all, but I looked up and there was one chicken perched in a tree. I climbed up and took it in my hand – the poor chicken was trembling.

It transpired that a fox had got through the hole in the netting and had systematically killed forty-eight chickens. A week later, one of our employees was using the wide, twenty-two-disk cultivator to cut the soil and tall grass when he saw the fox. The fox did not know that the cultivator was much wider than the tractor and as he squatted in the grass waiting for it to pass, the cultivator went over him and killed him.

I cannot recall what happened to the sole surviving chicken, but a year or so later I saw some young turkeys in the window of the egg-packing factory. Again, I could not resist the challenge so I bought six poults (young turkeys) and went about rearing them. They were doing very well when somehow two disappeared. We used wire in making timber cases and we would leave the wire on the lawn. It turned out that two turkeys somehow managed to get under a heap of wire and could not get out, but at least their predicament was more easily solved than that of the chickens!

Turkeys are very friendly birds and when our oldest daughter, Leah, was around three years old she would walk into the yard and the turkeys would surround her. One day, they even managed to get to the sandwich she was eating, so after that when Leah would appear, they would go up to her looking for food. She grew very fond of them and they would walk along with her in a most friendly way. One day we decided to have a turkey for *Shabbos* dinner, so my father purposely walked far away from the house to kill it. Unfortunately he did not notice that Leah was following him. She came home looking upset but saying nothing. It was not till some time later, when she was in Melbourne visiting her maternal grandmother, that she burst out saying, '*Zeide* is a naughty man because he hurt my turkey!'

As well as chickens and turkeys, we also had some ducks in the farmyard for a while. As our trusted employee Angelo was driving the tractor in the orchard one day, he passed a ditch and noticed a wild duck taking off in flight. He went to investigate and found a nest with twelve eggs in it. He kept watching the nest and saw one day that the mother had gone to feed. She had covered the eggs with a thick layer of down that she had plucked from her chest to keep the eggs warm while she was away. Angelo calculated that the eggs were not far from hatching so he took them from the nest and put them under a clucky hen. In only a few days, twelve wild ducklings had hatched. The mother hen took them for a walk and they headed straight for the water, which of course for them was natural. They quickly got into the water and swam away, leaving the poor mother hen jumping up and down, not knowing what to do. It was indeed pitiful to see her so distressed!

The ducklings finally came out of the water and went back with the mother hen to eat their feed. Angelo kept them in an enclosure for a week after that, but four of them escaped and flew away. The remaining eight stayed with their foster mother until they too flew off, once again leaving the mother hen bewildered.

A Bantam rooster

My four-legged friends

I have found that people either love horses or are indifferent to them and I am definitely a horse lover! As a result, I would like to digress a little to tell you something about the horses in our lives, both when I was young and in later years.

As I was growing up we had neither cars nor trucks. Horses were not only our means of transport, but were also the power units in the orchards. Up until 1936, when my father purchased the first tractor, all the haulage, cultivation and spraying of the fruit trees was done with horse power. Even as we acquired cars and trucks, horses continued to play an important role on the orchards.

We had a part-thoroughbred horse called Dowker, which my father had bought for my brother Judah. When Judah was conscripted into the army after World War I, Father thought that rather than going the hard way as a foot slogger, it would be easier to do his training on a horse. As part of his training, Judah's captain ordered his platoon to charge at a fairly wide ditch. The captain was in the lead and none of the horses attempted to jump, with the exception of Dowker! Another time, at an official function, all the horses were in line but Dowker would not stand still. The captain rebuked Judah, asking him to keep his horse still. He then ordered Judah to dismount and got on Dowker, but was thrown off a few seconds later. Getting up from the ground, the captain conceded that Judah was not at fault.

In the early 1930s, when Judah had left the army and Dowker was old and slow, he would take my brother Dave and sisters Sarah and Freda to school.

The next horse I remember was Prince, an old and reliable horse my father could always count on. Father would go to the township to collect the mail and see customers and sometimes the bank manager. The unmade road from our house to the made road could be very muddy and if the car was unable to make it, he would take old Prince. Prince would be hitched to the front of the car without a rein, as he worked by command and knew exactly what he had to do. As soon as the car's wheels would spin and the motor revved up, Prince knew he had to put his head down. He would strain to keep the car moving as far as the synagogue, which was on the corner of the surfaced road and the unmade road. When he finally reached the synagogue, he was unhitched and put into the synagogue yard, where he waited for my father's return to get the car back home.

On the day that Phar Lap (the famous Australian race horse) died in the United States of America, we found out as soon as we left school, so all the way home we sang, 'Phar Lap's dead, he died for want of bread.' When we reached the unmade road, which was nothing but slush and mud, we came upon Joina, our Italian employee, and the horse-drawn lorry. The lorry, with three horses and a load of box-making timber, was stuck to the axles in the mud. My father, who was a keen horseman, only bought the best horses, and one of the three was a big strong chestnut, an eye-pleasing horse he

47

named King. King was a cunning animal and as the other two horses strained and tried to move the heavy load, King did not attempt to do his part.

We stood watching, wondering if Joina would succeed in moving the lorry, but he had run out of patience. Here were two horses doing their utmost with King just refusing to help. Joina got off the lorry, unhitched King, took one of his pulling chains and used it to tie the horse to the lorry. He then took the other chain, doubling it up and thrashing him, saying, 'You blooda basta!' I stood in fright, thinking he was going to kill him. He then put the horse in his place beside the other horse and said, 'Gid up, you blooda basta!' I can still hear him yelling 'you blooda basta' at the horse. Apparently Joina knew what he was doing because after that outburst King put everything he had into the job. He took off like an Olympic sprinter out of the blocks and the three horses were then able to move the lorry and bring the load home.

One Passover, Dave 'stole' the *affikomen* and refused to give it back to my father until he promised he would buy a younger, faster pony. My father agreed and Dave searched for weeks on end until he found a young chestnut gelding and named him Phar Lap. Phar Lap seemed just what was required. He had no vices, was quite fast and, when harnessing or unharnessing him, he knew exactly when to move. So exact was he in his movements that one day, the assistant headmaster of Shepp (Shepparton) High School was watching Dave and congratulated him on the coordination and speed the horse had with its master.

Time went by and Dave and Sarah moved to Melbourne for their university education. Phar Lap was left in the yard 'unemployed'. One day, with nothing to do, I decided I would go for a ride. I caught him, took him out the front gate and jumped on to his back. No sooner was I on him than he reared up and slid me off, over his rump, so that I finished up on the grass behind him. He soon got into the swing of things and every time I jumped on, up he would go and deposit me on the grass. I think he enjoyed the fun of seeing me on the ground after every attempt, although he never lashed out with his two back legs and hurt me when I slid off him. After my sixth attempt, my sister-in-law, who lived on the property, came out and screamed at me, 'You'll get killed!' I continued trying for another twelve or so times until I finally gave up and took him back to the yard where his feed was waiting for him.

After that I had no more problems, as I realised he would cooperate as long as he had been fed. I used to come home from school, and Mother had a freshly baked yeast or sponge cake waiting with a cup of milk. As soon as I had had my snack, I would run out, grab the bridle and, bareback, I would take off with Phar Lap and Sailor on a little excursion. My father did not permit me to use a saddle because, a few years earlier, Dave had fallen off Dowker and had been dragged along the ground. Fortunately Joina saw him and I remember him running as hard as he could on to the road to stop the horse. At least if you fell off without a saddle, you would fall off cleanly.

Phar Lap had nothing else to do but go for a run and both he and Sailor enjoyed our outings. For me it was the highlight of my day and I would ride for ages. In time the muscles in my thighs developed so I could almost ride standing upright. One day, as I raced to the door, Mother called out, 'Where are you going?' She knew perfectly well, but she told me not to go out, trying to minimise the hurt she knew I was about to experience. 'Father sold Phar Lap today,' she said. You can imagine how the bottom dropped out of my world.

As you may have gathered, I was more the outdoor type than the studious type, be it secular studies or learning *Torah*. My father had a hard job to sit me down to learn, but here I must say, with all due respect, that he did not get his sums right. If he had said to me that I could keep my pony as long as I put in time daily to study, I would have seized the opportunity. It is hard to imagine the joy I had in going for my ride and the chagrin I felt when it was not to be any more. It hurt so much that I turned my back on looking at any horse for some time.

One day, as I was having my afternoon snack, Mother told me that there were men outside near the house spraying the fruit trees, using a horse which they had on trial to see if it was suitable to buy. She asked me to go out and see what I thought of it.

With spraying against moths or fungus, it is normal to order the horse to stop and go at regular intervals, so that each tree can be sprayed. As I watched this new horse, I noticed that every time he was called upon to move forward, he would shuffle around, mark time, then put his weight into his collar and move on. I went home and reported back to my mother, whereupon she asked my father to go and have a look. It was obvious the horse had an injury to his shoulder, so it was returned to its owner, Mr Logan, who had to have him destroyed. It turned out that the injury was the result of a serious accident.

Mr Logan, an Irishman who knew a bit about animals, was none too pleased about our decision. By the way, Mr

Logan was one of the few remaining survivors of the *Titanic*. The *Titanic* sank in 1912 and I asked him one day what he remembered of it. This is what he said:

Before the *Titanic* went out on its maiden voyage they were advertising for all sorts of people to work on the ship. I was a very young lad of fifteen and I applied to be a bellboy. I was accepted and when the ship, as you know, came across an iceberg, it should have almost stopped, but the captain, believing his ship was unsinkable, ordered it straight ahead. Well, history proved the captain wrong. There was panic on board and the stern was already high up in the air. They were screaming from the top of the ship to come up, as lifeboats were going out with hardly anyone in them. So, using the rails, I clambered up to the top of the ship and sat myself in a lifeboat. There was still room for many more people, but people were scared to attempt the steep climb up to the lifeboats. I was one of the lucky ones who made it.

Some time after the episode of the injured horse, a considerable amount of white powder was noticed on the grass along the road. No one paid much attention to it, however, until a cow died. The cow belonged to our neighbours, a very large family who lived on a one-hectare block on the corner of our lane, and it provided the family with much-needed milk. Our draught horses would also feed on the grass along the road after working in the orchards, ending up in the yard of another little property we owned to be fed, watered and sheltered overnight. One day, we also lost two horses. It was obvious that the poison – which turned out to be arsenic – had been deliberately spread. Who did it? Well, I'm not a detective, but it wasn't hard to work out who it was!

The loss of their cow was indeed a blow to our neighbour and his large family, as our loss was to us. For us to lose two horses then was a financial blow, but our neighbours lost an important source of food.

When our horses were let out after work and made their way to the little yard where they were fed, they would go at full gallop. One of the horses was Bon, an animal with brains and a lead horse of the lorry. Bon was the third horse up front, knowing exactly how to steer the lorry up close to the railway track, to bring timber for boxes home or take fruit to the station to be sent to Albury and then on to Sydney.

It so happened that one day the horses were let loose to go to their night quarters up the road. They came out of the yard at full gallop, turning at a right angle on to the road. I was only four but I can still remember this very clearly. There was Sam, my younger brother, then about one-and-a-half years old, sitting in his nappies in the middle of the road, right in the path of the galloping horses. Bon, the leader, stopped, put his head down and sniffed Sam as he carefully walked around him. The other horses, following their leader, did the same.

Quite a few years later, a fellow came to our property with a draught horse he wanted to sell, an unbroken brumby from the Barmah Forest on the Murray River. We bought him and called him Nugget. After he was broken in, he turned out to be an exceptional horse, tackling every job with great success, including bringing the fruit in from the orchard on the lorry. One day, Nugget and I were bringing the fruit home from the orchard. The going was hard, as the ground was wet, and tall, wild millet grew between the trees. Suddenly Nugget jumped sideways and did not move. I got off the lorry very carefully, expecting a snake in the grass, but it turned out to be one of the itinerant fruit pickers sound asleep in our path. If it were not for Nugget's keen sense of observation I would have run straight over the top of him and that would have been the end of him!

Not long after this, the Dunera boys came out of internment camp. Five or six came to live in a Jewish Welfare Society (now Jewish Care) hostel for workers in Shepparton and worked in our orchard. Haim, one of these boys, had the task of taking the empty boxes into the orchard to be filled, then bringing the filled boxes back to the shed. Nugget was so good at working with Haim and Haim cared for him lovingly.

One day, Haim walked back to the shed and reported that the lorry was loaded but Nugget was refusing to pull it. I went into the orchard and tried to get him going, but although he tried, he just stopped and looked around at me. I immediately saw the problem. He was overworked and overtired, so Haim unyoked him, brought him home and took another horse. After a week's spell, Nugget was back, hard at work again.

Another time one of the boys who came down every year from Queensland was bringing in a load of fruit. (We had four or five workers during the winter months but hired an extra twenty-five or thirty fruit pickers and sorters in summer.) The ground was soft and the going was particularly hard and the young fellow said that Nugget refused to pull the lorry. When I asked if he had hit him, he replied that he had belted him. Well, I knew that if you were in any way cruel to him, he would refuse to work. I went up to the orchard, and Nugget turned towards the driver, saying in horse language, 'You can do it yourself!' Ordering the driver to walk away, I went up to Nugget, looked in the grass for a ripe pear, gave it to him, scratched him under the chin and said gently, 'Get up.' Away he went, no problem at all!

Nugget worked until he was around twenty. We then retired him and let him live out his life. He had earned a nice retirement and died at thirty-three years old, which is extremely old for a horse. Other horses past working age were sent to the horse sale, where they were bought for feed for the lions and tigers in the zoo, but not Nugget.

By 1952, our work was mechanised and we had no horses. By that time, I had a bad hip and walking was agony. I would lift up my trouser leg and pull my leg along, but in winter, wearing my rubber boots, pulling my leg through the mud in the orchards was all but impossible. I decided I needed a horse to help me, so I had a horse float built and went to Melbourne to buy a horse.

I bought an Anglo-Arab horse called Silver, whose previous job had been to lead winning racehorses at Flemington Race Course. By that stage my family was living in East St Kilda, so I brought him there on a Sunday, planning to take him to Shepparton the next day. When I tied him to a lamp post outside our place, I discovered that he was a 'puller'; that is, he would pull backwards with all his strength to get free. The only way I could get him to move forward in order to untie him from the post was to whip him across the rump so he jumped forward. Once I had done this I decided to put him in the garage, which had a door that lifted upwards, but again he said no!

My wife, Ruth, had gone to a lot of trouble to prepare dinner and as it took me so long to get Silver into the garage, she was becoming exasperated too. I was at odds to know what to do, so in desperation, I grabbed Silver by the ear, giving him a lecture about his parents, which was none too complimentary. Miracle of miracles, he then walked straight into the garage, where I was able to leave him with food and water. The next day I put him in the float and we drove back to Shepparton.

Before mounting Silver for the first time I told him that if he helped me through the mud, I would reward him by taking him for a ride on the hard metal roads. After our difficult beginning, we got on very well and he was a great help! I would also take the children for rides on him as he was very gentle. Once, when my daughter Naomi was three and I was taking her for a ride, he took little steps and turned around ever so gently, aware that he had a baby on his back. If I hadn't seen it, I wouldn't have believed a horse could be so intelligent.

Pure Arab foals were very valuable, so I began to breed horses as an extra source of income. I bought an Arab mare and reared its nine foals. To make sure that they too did not become pullers, I decided to follow a technique which I had heard about. I prepared myself with a good sharp knife and a thin piece of flat board, tying the rope with a slip knot around the horse's neck and putting the board between the rope and his neck. The harder the horse pulled, the tighter the rope would become around his neck, cutting off his air supply. I would leave him gasping for breath, making sure he did not choke. When he was all but choking, I would cut the rope so that he was free to breathe again, the board preventing the horse from being injured. From this, the horse learnt that pulling back was not a good idea.

Aaron with a Palomina colt, 1961

Etzyona and her colt foal, 1982

High School

Orrvale State School went up to Grade 8 and from there we went on to Shepparton High School, which offered the last four years of secondary school – Forms 3,4, 5 and 6 (now Years 9–12). Form 5 was Matriculation and Form 6 was Honours. Most of the pupils who went to Orrvale State School finished school after Grade 8.

I went off to high school in 1934, in my *bar mitzvah* year. We went by bicycle, so my aim was to have a racing bike. By then our family was making fruit boxes and was the biggest supplier to orchardists in the district. In the summer holidays, before I started high school, I had the opportunity to work in the box-making business, nailing up the boxes. I worked as much as I could, managing to earn five pounds three shillings ($10.30), a large amount to me but not enough to buy the bike I wanted. The week before school started, my father took me into a cycle shop in Shepparton and told me to pick out the bike I liked. I immediately walked up to the racing bike, but it was nine pounds ten shillings ($19). My father bargained with the owner and finally got it for seven pounds fifteen shillings ($15.50). I had not earned that much, but my father said I had tried hard so he gave me the balance. I was indeed happy and proud of my hard-earned wheels.

A few years later the old high school in the centre of

Shepparton had become too small. A new school was being built one-and-a-half kilometres away from the existing one and the state school was to move into the old high school. When the time came to shift out of the old school, the teacher organised a procession of students to ride along in pairs. We had to ride with one hand on the shoulder of the student with whom we were paired. With a celebratory torch, we were to proceed to the newly built school. We had several practice rides before the actual event and on one of these, we were riding along when the teacher called a halt. To dismount I would kick the pedal, sending the bike forward while I jumped off backwards, catching the bike seat. I did this, but this time I missed, catching the seat as it went under me, so my bike careered down the road. Mr Daws, the teacher in charge, called out, 'Hold everything, Aaron's bike has bolted!' Apart from this mishap, everything went according to plan.

The old school high school had lawns and a flower garden. The boys had one lawn and the girls had the other, separated by a path and the flowerbed. One day, our class was walking along the path, going from one classroom to another when a fellow as tall as I was walked past and gave me a mighty push. He managed to push me on to the freshly dug flower bed in front of the girls' section of lawn.

How the girls laughed and enjoyed the joke, but I did not! I got up, walked up to this smart guy and gave him one mighty slap across his face. So hard did I hit him that I sprained my thumb. His immediate reaction was to have it out with boxing gloves. I excused myself, explaining that I had sprained my thumb, but told him 'it would keep'.

After about a month, my 'pushy' friend demanded that

the unfinished episode be settled with the gloves. At morning recess we went outside, put on the boxing gloves and faced up, surrounded by a large ring of boys looking forward to the match. We went at it flat out and he hit me so that I went backwards, hitting myself behind the ear on a large pine tree. I was stunned, not knowing where I was, and my arms were so tired I could no longer punch. Once again, however, my angel came along and asked what was wrong with my legs. Hearing the message, I put my fists out in front of me and squatted down. With the force of flexing my knees I was able to break through his guard and land him with a hefty punch on his nose, his bleeding nose ending the fight. He nose bled for so long that his parents were telephoned and he was taken home. He was back at school in a few days and we finished up as good friends.

One day I got the strap for breaking a school rule, which stated that you were not to go into the classroom after class was dismissed. As I was walking past the room one day, one young fellow grabbed my cap and threw it into the room through the window. Jewish law states that males must not eat unless their heads are covered, so I wasn't going to eat without my cap. As I walked into the room to retrieve it, the teacher called me over and gave me the strap. This punishment ruled me out from ever being appointed a prefect.

I also recall getting into trouble during the 1937 mid-term exams. As we were waiting to go in to the classroom to sit for the science exam, Alan Montgomery, a lovely fellow, one of nature's gentlemen (who incidentally, was killed during World War II) told me that he hadn't bothered to study one of the topics. I told him I was as sure as one can possibly be that that it would be a question on the paper and suggested that he study it in the five minutes we had left before the exam.

Once in the exam room, I was sitting on one side of the room and he was on the other, with about six rows of desks between us. We looked at the paper and both looked up and smiled at each other. My smile said 'I told you it would be on the paper' and his said 'thank you for telling me'. At that moment a teacher passed by in the corridor. Her name was Miss McNaughton, but we used to call her 'Snucker' because she was a sneak. When she saw us smiling at each other, she came into the classroom and told Miss Noble, the teacher who was supervising the exam, that she had seen Alan and me talking to each other. She also suggested our exam papers should be cancelled. Miss Noble's response was that she was the supervisor and did not see anything of the sort. She knew we had not been talking to each other and refused to cancel our papers. Miss McNaughton continued to argue the point, before walking away without getting her way.

This exam incident reminds me of another that happened around exam time. It was *Tisha Ba'av* and we had all been to synagogue in the morning. It is usual not to do any work until lunch time, but the exams were looming and I was behind with my school work, so I went to school in the afternoon. Sam and his friend were not as concerned about their studies and were riding around town on their bikes. The headmaster happened to see them and called them in the next day to ask why they had not been at school. I was called in too, although I did not know why. I must have provided him with a satisfactory explanation, however, as the others were let off without any punishment.

Whilst on the subject of Sam's friend, this boy's locker happened to be underneath mine at school. One day, as we were both at our lockers, he complained of a pain in his stomach. I asked if he could ride his bike and when he said he could, I told him to go to the doctor, who wasn't far from the school. He did so, but the doctor wasn't there and the nurse told him to go home and take 'a good dose of salts'. Sure enough, he had appendicitis and his appendix burst. Sadly he died of peritonitis within seven days. I did what I thought was best and was not responsible for the nurse's advice, but still feel guilty that I had somehow contributed to his demise.

In 1937 the Jewish Welfare Society bought a large parcel of land in the Shepparton area, which was settled by some six Jewish families. Orchards were planted, houses built and the new arrivals settled in. As can easily happen, there were arguments over minor things. One day, I was in class when the headmaster's secretary called for me to come into the headmaster's office. I came in as an interpreter from Yiddish to English. As we only spoke Yiddish at home, at my father's insistence, we all spoke it fluently.

In the headmaster's office was the son of one of the settlers, who looked like he had been belted up, and another man from this subdivision, who must have followed him to school. The two families lived side by side and had to use a common bridge over the canal to reach the road. Each claimed to be the owner of the bridge. They were swearing at each other in a language I had never heard before. In my role as interpreter, I invented a story about a horse, which had nothing to do with what they were saying, and it did not take the headmaster long to see that I was fabricating. He tried to resolve it by telling me to explain that in this country it is not customary to go round belting up people and suggested that they should go to the police if the disagreement was serious.

Even in peaceful Shepparton news reached us of growing anti-Semitism in Europe. In 1938, particularly at the time of *Kristallnacht,* the newspaper was full of the treatment the Jews were experiencing in Germany. One day as we were lined up outside the classroom ready to enter (the deputy headmaster would blow his whistle twice – once to get ready and again as a signal for us to march into our classroom), a hefty fellow, of German descent and built like a tank, was in front of me in the line. He turned around, calling me a 'Jewish viper'. I had to show him he was not in Germany, so I stepped out of line, stood beside him, closed my fist and hit him as hard as I could where it hurt most – on the upper part of the arm, below the shoulder. The teacher in charge, who saw all this and knew perfectly well what it was all about, merely said, 'Aaron, step back into line and prepare to go into the classroom.'

This incident reminds me of the sad story of Rabbi Goldberg, who came to Shepparton to work as the *shochet* and *melamed* for the Jewish community. Rabbi Goldberg, who was a relative of Nehemia Rosenbaum, one of the founding settlers, arrived from Poland around 1937. He stayed with the Rosenbaums and was provided with a jinker and pony he had to look after. It was a far cry from his previous life in a Polish town. Rabbi Goldberg was a mathematical genius. He would ask us to write down two lines of figures, one beneath the other. He would then multiply the two lines, carrying all the figures in his head. My brother Sam was required to use logarithms to work out some of his maths problems and when

Rabbi Goldberg saw him struggling, he asked Sam to explain what he had to do. Rabbi Goldberg then solved the problem in his head. When Sam told his teacher the next day, the teacher didn't believe it was possible!

Rabbi Goldberg had come to Australia leaving his wife and five children behind in Poland. My father felt that, in view of the situation in Europe, Rabbi Goldberg should bring his family to Australia, and offered to help him. The rabbi declined as he felt that the 'desert of *Torah*' that was Australia was not something to which he wanted to bring his family. In 1939, the situation had become intolerable for the Jewish people and one day there was a photo of some Jews fleeing their homes. Amongst the victims, the rabbi recognised one of his sons. War broke out and the rabbi, realising his family was trapped, suffered a mental breakdown. He never fully recovered and when he passed away he was buried at Springvale Cemetery, next to the grave of Shochet Glick, who had also been the *shochet* in Shepparton earlier in the twentieth century.

Shepparton High School, 1936, with Aaron back row centre

Joining the workforce

I left school when I finished Form 5 in 1938 and I stayed on the orchard, working for the family company and learning every aspect of work on the orchard. By then we had moved out of the horse age and were using trucks and tractors.

The practice then was to cultivate by continually turning the soil. My brother Judah, seeing how slow this process was, decided to buy a crawler tractor and a large tandem disc cultivator. A tandem cultivator has twenty-two disc plates, half running in front and half behind, so it covered far more ground than the old horse-drawn plough. I soon graduated to driving the tractor and cultivator and could cover a considerable amount of area in a relatively short period of time.

One day I was working on the home block, going along quite nicely, when a squeak developed in the cultivator. I kept glancing backwards, concentrating on keeping the tractor going in a straight line so as not to run into the butts of the fruit trees. Suddenly, whilst I was looking behind me, a heavy apricot branch whacked me across the chest. Some mighty quick thinking was called for, as the tractor was very powerful and I found myself sitting in the driver's seat with the back of the seat – a steel plate – wedged into my back. I had to stop the tractor but found I could not reach the hand clutch in front of me. The tractor was moving forward and I couldn't stop it!

Fortunately I was able to think quickly and immediately used my foot to kick the clutch forward. Realising that the steel of the clutch was shiny and slippery, I had the presence of mind to turn my boot so that if the sole slipped, the heel would give me a second chance. I managed to stop the tractor, but was still pinned to the seat behind me, with the gear stick between my knees. As the clutch was disengaged, I took the gear lever and put it in reverse, using the toe of my boot to bring the clutch lever back ever so gently till I felt a movement. Fortunately I was able to take the tractor back far enough to release myself from being pinned between the branch and the tractor seat.

It seems the workers responsible for pruning had decided to leave that huge limb, but I didn't feel quite so sympathetic! The next run down the row of trees brought me close to the shed so I went in and picked up a pruning saw. When I came back up the row to my would-be assassin, I cut off the heavy limb and dragged it out of the way to the rubbish dump.

Around this time I obtained my driver's license. In my test the police remarked that I handled the car well, but I had been driving the car since I was fifteen. (Road rules were not as strict as they are today and there was not nearly as much traffic). I would drive to other Jewish families to collect money so my father could pay the rabbi, as well as to collect Jewish boys to come to synagogue for *Yom Tov*. Jewish families in Europe had sent their children to Australia to escape the growing anti-Semitism and the Jewish Welfare Society had placed several of these children on farms around Victoria so they could learn to be farmers. As these boys were living with non-Jewish families, Father sent me out by car to bring them to Shepparton to be amongst Jewish people. My friend Cliff Wright came with me. Cliff had been my very close friend in high school and we remained friends. Incidentally, Cliff's older sister worked in the chemist shop and my father used to say that Cliff's sister 'must come from Jewish people'. As it happened, Cliff told me one day that his great-grandmother was Jewish!

* * *

I moved to Melbourne in 1939 and lived with my sisters and their families. I attended Melbourne University on Monday and Tuesday to study commerce (including geography, which I enjoyed) and worked from Wednesday to Friday at the family timber mill in Narbethong. My brothers wanted to send an old Diamond T truck from the mill to Shepparton, as it was too old to use at the mill but would be useful for taking fruit to the cannery.

I was given the job of driving the truck back to Shepparton. It was a very hot day in December and Abe Weinstock was coming with me. Abe was a student who was coming to Shepparton to earn money picking fruit. We were carrying about three tonnes of case-making material. We left an hour after daybreak and, as we were driving, the motor became tight and hot and the petrol started vaporising. As we were coming up Cathedral Hill near Alexandra, the engine kept cutting out, so we poured some cold water on the carburettor to cool it down. When the motor cut out, the truck would roll backwards and Abe would put chocks of timber behind the wheels to stop the truck rolling back.

We managed to get to the top of the hill and continued very slowly until we reached Euroa. It was almost dark and as it was wartime, all the road signs had been removed, for fear of a Japanese invasion. Although I knew the way to Shepparton, I was not familiar with all the roads, so I headed in what I though was the right direction. When night fell, I tried to switch the truck's lights on but, lo and behold, they did not work! Fortunately the moonlight was bright and we drove on very slowly.

Just to make matters worse, the truck's brakes failed as well. Eventually we came to the Broken River, which had a bridge across it, but there was a sharp angle turn on to the bridge. With no brakes it was hard to steer and we could have ended up in the river. However, by standing up and leaning over the steering wheel, I was able to get more power into my arms and managed to steer the truck on to the bridge. We crossed the bridge and kept going, but I then missed the turn-off to the main highway. Luckily I recognised a church we used to pass and realised I had gone the wrong way. (This reminds me again of horses and their instinct of returning to the place where they were born. We had bought a horse not far from the church and if he got out of the yard, he would always head back there, taking all the other horses with him. At least we knew where to find them!)

There were several roads leading from the church and I knew which one to take to Shepparton. By this time, however, there was panic in the homesteads both in Shepparton and in Narbethong. It had been twelve hours since I had left Narbethong and my family in Shepparton and Narbethong had been in touch with each other and were worried that I had not appeared. My father and brother in Shepparton decided to head towards Euroa to look for me and agreed to phone my brothers in Narbethong if they found me. If not, my brothers in Narbethong would start looking for me along their end of the route.

I reached the synagogue near home, where I had to make a right-hand turn and continued on to Feiglin Road, the road to our homestead. My brother and father had just turned out of this road when they heard a truck and, sure enough, it was us. By this time we were completely and utterly exhausted. After eating and showering, we went to bed and it didn't take us long to get to sleep!

* * *

The family business was called M Feiglin & Sons. After establishing the orchards, its next venture – making fruit boxes – happened without any real planning. Before our family became involved, the timber used to make fruit boxes was transported by railroad to the box maker in Shepparton. One day, three carriage loads of timber had been damaged, so the box maker refused to take delivery. Instead, he left the timber in the hands of the stationmaster, who decided to put it out for tender. My brother Judah decided to put in a low tender and much to our surprise it was accepted, as the stationmaster just wanted to get rid of it.

Judah carted the timber back from the station, laid it out in piles of equal width and we made the boxes. My father then went out to get orders. We had made twelve hundred boxes with that first load, but my father came back with orders for five thousand, so he decided to go to the timber mills at Warburton to buy more. On the train, he was telling another passenger the reason for his trip and it just so happened that this passenger had a timber mill he was prepared to sell. My family bought the mill in Milgrove, which Judah ran. Once the timber was milled, it was transported to our property in Shepparton, where the boxes were made. Gradually the business grew and my brother Joseph, who was at university in Melbourne, joined Judah at the mill.

In 1939 there were bushfires raging in Victoria and our timber mills were right in their path. Although not required by law, my brothers had thought it necessary to provide protection against fires, so they had built a shelter. It was dug into the side of a hill with a narrow entry where you could hang a wet blanket to keep the smoke from coming in. Joseph and Judah were at the timber mill in 1939 when the fire came down over the Black Spur like an express train. It came so fast that Joe only had time to grab the bag he always brought from Melbourne with his books, *tallis* and *tefillin* and rush for the shelter. He and Judah and eight employees who were at the mill at the time all crowded in and were there for around fifteen hours until the fires passed.

My brother-in-law, Aaron Kaploun, who was also at the mill, was able to pick up all our employees' wives by car and head towards Narbethong. He sped along the road with the fires bearing down and the air filled with thick smoke, skidding and cutting corners to get to the safety of a large, empty paddock as quickly as possible. Sadly, another man and his wife and little daughter were not so fortunate as they tried to escape by car and died tragically when a burning log fell across their path.

The blacksmith, who was looking after the fourteen horses we had at the mill, ran past the corral and let the horses out. These horses had more brains than some of the people around them. A number of people in adjoining mills jumped into large water tanks, thinking they would be safe there, but the water boiled and they perished. Our mill was near the Acheron River, so the horses headed for the river and jumped in, following the river downstream until they found a deep hole. There they sheltered until the fire passed, returning to the mill unharmed.

My parents, Sam and I were in Shepparton at the time and we had no way of contacting my brothers. We had heard the news about the fires and naturally were beside ourselves with worry. Eventually Joseph and Judah were able to telephone us to allay our fears. They also asked my parents to send a truckload of chaff as soon as they could, as the horses did not have any other food.

In 1941 I returned to Shepparton from Melbourne. The orchard was producing dried fruit for the army and the timber mill was busy manufacturing timber to be used in building army huts for the Pacific islands. As I mentioned earlier, although I had been called up, I was exempted from the army on the grounds of being involved in work necessary for the war effort.

One day, I was coming home from the railway station with a truckload of timber. I had a coil of rope sitting on the running board and was worried I would lose it, so I picked it up to put it in the cabin. I was going very slowly but the rope rolled around my fingers, got caught in the back wheel and tore off two fingers on my right hand. One of the Dunera boys was with me and he fainted! I stopped and hailed down a passing car and the driver took me to the doctor. It just happened that my father was also there as he had taken another Dunera boy to the doctor.

That day was Friday, 13 March. That morning when I had been collecting fruit from other orchardists to dry, one fellow warned me that I needed to be careful as it was the dreaded 'Friday the thirteenth'. I thought that was a lot of bunkum, but I ended up in hospital having surgery! There was a big argument between the surgeon and the anaesthetist, one wanting to remove my middle finger, which was such a mess, and the other believing that part of it could be saved. Fortunately, the one against removing it completely won out, and having part of my finger made a big difference to my life. It meant I was still able to write with my right hand, although I did become left-handed for many other things.

One day, several weeks after my accident, my arm was still in a sling, but I managed to drive with one hand. By then, many of the Dunera boys had been released from camp and were working on the orchards. Moishe Rabi, who had been interned when he was young and had been surrounded by uniformed people, had the fear of authority in his bones. When he was ready to leave camp, I was to drive and pick him up. As my school friend Cliff was on leave from the navy, I asked him to come along with me. When we arrived at the camp, Moishe came out to meet us, but froze when he saw a uniformed sailor. He soon thawed out and off we went to Shepparton, but it underlined for me what traumas these young men had experienced.

Moishe finally came to Melbourne, met a young lady from overseas and married. We have been friends from the time we met until this very day, sharing each other's *simchas* and getting on very well together.

When I was at home recovering from my operation, I was

reading the *Shepparton News* and saw that the Murray Valley irrigation system was being extended. There was land to be purchased in Yarroweah, near Cobram, and as we were short of land to grow peaches, I suggested to my father and brother that we take a drive to look around.

We drove to Cobram on a fine warm June day. Mr McDonald, a member of parliament, had orchards on land that had already been irrigated and we wanted to see them. When we stopped to ask for directions, we got into conversation with the man on the road; he wanted to know where we were from and if we were looking for a 'bit of dirt'. Instead of telling us how to find Mr McDonald, this Irishman took us four kilometres up the road to meet Bill Irwin.

Bill had one hundred and thirty hectares of land near the Murray River, about eight kilometres west of Cobram. His father had come by the land when the Government allowed people to peg out an area and buy it at a very nominal rate. Bill wanted to sell not only because he was getting on in years, but also because he preferred dry farming to the irrigation that had just been introduced. He was one of thirteen children – two girls and eleven boys. As the eldest boy had died soon after he was married, all the other boys had decided that marriage was not for them! When we met, Bill was living with one of his sisters.

We walked across the property and saw the beautiful soil and native pine trees on this virgin land. Mr Irwin was asking twelve pounds ten ($25) an acre. My father wanted to give him a cheque as a deposit, but Bill wanted us to come back the next day with the estate agent to finalise the sale.

We returned to Bill Irwin's the next morning with the agent

and with the Irishman, who felt responsible for brokering the sale and wanted to see it through to the end. Not content to just be an observer, he had to have a say just as we were about to finalise the deal, complaining sarcastically that we were not paying enough. Fortunately for us, Bill Irwin did not agree, thumping the table and exclaiming, 'No bloody fear. Twelve pound ten is my price and that's all I want!'

Although officially in Yarroweah, we always referred to the property as 'Cobram'. I was the first of the family to work there and I would stay overnight at the house there. I planted tomatoes in the first year and also helped to remove the pine trees, using a horse to load them on to the truck and taking them into Cobram, where they were cut into timber. I then brought the timber back and we used it to build a house for a manager. Later, Abraham and I would travel the sixty kilometres to and from Shepparton every day with a carload of workers who planted and tended the orchards. We later also employed a manager, who lived in the house, and I would camp in the little hut next door. It had a bed and a small stove fuelled by methylated spirits on which I was able to cook eggs and boil water for tea.

Around 1943 I planted tomatoes there as food for the war effort. I picked up a truckload of several thousand seedlings from Mr McArthur in Shepparton and headed off to Cobram with four Dunera boys to plant them. I gave each of them a handful of seedlings and showed the boys how to plant them in lines. One fellow was particularly enthusiastic and raced back to tell me he was finished before anyone else, but when I saw what he had done, lo and behold, he had the roots in the air and the leaves in the ground!

Despite his efforts, our crop was a great success and when the tomatoes were ripe, the fields were a sea of red. The only problem was that we needed the Dunera boys on the orchards in Shepparton and labour was almost impossible to obtain during wartime in Yarroweah. Luckily, the men stationed at the big air force base at Tocumwal had two and a half hours off in the middle of the day. Their base was twenty kilometres away, on the other side of the river in New South Wales, and I would drive out there to pick up as many as I could fit into the car. They did a good job but they were unable to pick the whole crop and many tomatoes rotted on the ground.

* * *

When I was supervising the work on the orchards in Cobram I heard about a professional fisherman in Cobrawonga, half way between Cobram and Yarrawonga. I would drive to his place in the Diamond T truck to buy the Murray cod he caught in a big billabong adjoining the Murray River. As there was very little petrol available during the war, the truck had a gas producer which burnt charcoal to produce fuel. To get going, you had to tip charcoal into the burner at the side of the truck; on longer drives, you would have to stop and add more charcoal, producing a great whoosh of fire and smoke when the lid of the burner was lifted.

The first time I bought fish at Cobrawonga, I paid the fisherman with cash, but I soon found out he was a hopeless alcoholic, so I would bring him a bottle of whisky as well. Sometimes I would buy a fish weighing over twenty kilograms; sometimes two, around nine or ten kilos, usually on a Thursday so Mother would have them for *Shabbos*.

When the fisherman caught large, fatty fish, he would

tether them on cords to limit their food intake. They would lose their blubber, making them suitable for eating, and he would sell them to local cafes. If I arrived and he was too drunk to know I was there, I would inspect the tethered fish and take what I wanted. I would leave however much money I thought appropriate, plus a bottle of whisky, take my fish and go.

The fisherman used drum nets to catch fish (a practise which is illegal today, but then he had a license). One day, when he was in better shape, we went out in his boat together. He stopped in the middle of the river, pulled up one of his nets and there was a beautiful eight or nine kilo cod. He put it in the boat and we went across to the other side of the river – the New South Wales side – where he was tethering a whole lot of fish. He pointed out a cord which he told me to pull, so I stood up and kept pulling until a huge fish appeared. It was so big that it looked like a pig and turned out to weigh almost a hundred and ten kilos!

The Murray River was renowned for its cod. One day I went out with my friend Cliff, who was on leave from the navy. It was late spring or early summer, when the Murray cod spawn. Cliff and I were having lunch on the river bank when masses of tiny Murray cod swam past. Tens of thousands would probably be an underestimate of their numbers. Murray cod are cannibals and the smaller fish provide food for the larger fish. Once I purchased a fish which would have weighed around fifteen kilos and it had a half kilo fish stuck in its throat!

The Murray River could be very treacherous. One day, I was checking our orchards in Cobram and all was going well, so

I decided to drive across the river to Tocumwal to visit some Jewish boys who were working there. At that time there was a single-gauge railway line running from Melbourne to the border and a different gauge line from the border to Sydney. Several Jewish boys were working there, shifting goods from the Victorian trains to the New South Wales trains so that they could be transported to Sydney. It was a hot day and I arrived at Tocumwal around half past four in the afternoon. I went to the boys' camp, but could see something serious had taken place. I soon found out that the boys had gone for a swim in the Murray River and had been caught in a whirlpool, for which the Murray is notorious. Sadly, three boys were drowned that day.

Coming back to the subject of fish, many years later when my granddaughter Channah was in Prep at the age of six, it came to 'Show and Tell' and she could not wait to tell her fish story. Three or four weeks earlier, a professional fisherman, who had worked for our company when he was a lad, came to see me with an eleven-kilo Murray cod. It reminded me of my mother and the fish I would buy her for the Sabbath and *Yom Tov*, so I bought it for old time's sake. Channah stood up in front of her class and told them her *Zeide* had bought a fish in Shepparton that was 'so big', stretching her arms out as far as she could. The teacher was not impressed and told Channah to sit down, but Channah picked up the disbelief in her voice and was deeply hurt. Fortunately I had stored the fish in the freezer, so we took a photo of Channah trying to hold it. It was so big that her father had to stand behind her taking its weight. Channah took the photo to school and showed it to her teacher, who apologized immediately, making her a very happy little girl.

At our Cobram property there were two large sand dunes which were suitable for growing citrus. As citrus growing was something that was new to me, I decided to go to Mildura to learn about it. It was 1957 and there I met a man by the name of Jock Duncan, who had a two-thousand-hectare property he was trying to sell. When I came back to Melbourne I told my brothers about it and we were all enthusiastic about buying it. Around the same time I read in *The Age* that there was thirty-two hectares of land for sale in Preston. I was also enthusiastic about buying this land as I thought it would be very profitable, but I was overruled on the grounds that the Feiglins knew much more about fruit growing than suburban real estate. That land in Preston ended up being worth millions! Fruit growing did not make us such huge profits, but we did manage to keep our heads above water.

We bought Jock Duncan's land in Mildura and planted citrus and grapes. A manager ran the property and my brother Dave oversaw its operation, commuting the over-five-hundred kilometres from Melbourne by air every two or three weeks.

* * *

In 1941, when one of my sisters was getting married, my mother went to Melbourne to organise the wedding. At that stage there was a big army base at Puckapunyal, about eighty kilometres from our place. There was a serious throat infection raging at the time, known as 'Pucka throat', which I had the misfortune to catch. I was so ill that our family doctor came to visit me three times in one day. Under the doctor's care and with medication and G-d's help, I pulled through, but Father decided to send me to Melbourne so that Mother could look after me.

Father packed me up and put me and my suitcase on the train to Melbourne. When I arrived, I had to catch the Nicholson Street cable tram from the station. As the tram stopped two kilometres from my sister's place, I had to walk the rest of the way and I can still so well recall that walk! I was so weak that I had to rest every ten minutes in order to keep going. I finally managed to drag myself to 15 King Street, North Fitzroy. My mother took one look at me, rushed up, took me by the arm and sat me down in a chair, before hastily preparing a nourishing meal for me. I was pale and had lost so much weight I must have looked like a scarecrow. My mother's loving care helped, but it took another eight months before I was able even to think about doing anything slightly strenuous, like climbing up a ladder.

As the war continued, we heard that there were around a million American soldiers stationed in Victoria. Many were in camps between Seymour and Nagambie, training in preparation to take part in fighting in the Pacific. One day, when my father and I were at the Shepparton railway station, a train full of American soldiers was waiting to depart. As we walked along the platform, one soldier jumped out of his carriage, threw his arms around my father and said, 'Reb Yid, give me a brocha.' My father replied, 'You should come back well and healthy.'

We worked very hard during the war, with two dehydrators working night and day to dry fruit for the army. We were supervised by an American army captain whose job was to make sure we produced the maximum amount of dried fruit possible. He happened to be Jewish, but one Saturday morning he turned up and wondered why we weren't working. My father patiently explained that we worked until sundown on Friday and began again after sunset on Saturday, but we never worked on *Shabbos*. Unfortunately, he didn't know much more about Judaism than *prakes* and *kreplach,* although I'm sure we helped to expand his knowledge!

Jewish refugee workers on the orchard, 1937

The crawler tractor

Duneera boys, around 1941

A fine example of a
Murray cod, around 18
kilograms, with Mervyn
Smith, former manager of
the Feiglin orchards
at right

Chana and the fish

By ship to Europe

Ihad always been interested in geography, so after World War II, I decided to go travelling. M Feiglin & Sons was then buying machinery in Sweden for cutting up logs, so I had an excuse to go to Europe to see how and where the machines were made. I booked my passage by boat from Melbourne to London and organised accommodation with an orthodox Jewish family by the name of Wechsler at 83 Lordship Park, North London.

My departure date was 3 July 1947. We were delayed by a strike of tugboat operators, but the *Astoris* finally left Station Pier in the late afternoon. The family came to farewell me and my nephew Lionel, who was then about three years old, asked his father if it was 'Uncle Aaron's ship'!

I shared a cabin with seven other men. One was a man whom I knew from Shepparton, who was going back to Czechoslovakia (now the Czech Republic), and another an Italian with whom we did business, as he had a fruit shop in Carlton. As we went through the heads at Port Phillip Bay, I called them all together to tell them that none of us must rob any of the others. However, I also suggested we should not allow anyone else into the cabin, as any strangers may not be as trustworthy. Everyone agreed to this.

We passed Adelaide and headed towards the Great Australian Bight, where I became seasick. At the beginning of the journey I was frightened that the ship might sink, but when I experience my first bout of seasickness, I was frightened it wouldn't! I was violently sick for the three and a half days it took to get through the Bight. I lay on my bed, only able to eat my mother's sponge cake, which I had stored under my bunk, and to have the occasional sip of water.

Finally we arrived in Fremantle. It was late Saturday night and some Jewish people came down to the boat to look after the Jewish passengers. One was a relation of my sister-in-law, who invited me to her home. Seeing how gaunt I looked, she offered to make me something to eat. She saw my hesitation but assured me that everything would be kosher. She made me a good meal of fried fish, which I not only needed but also enjoyed. The next day, before we left, I bought a large box of Granny Smith apples and another box of oranges. My mother had also made me two big tins of strudel, laced with plenty of oil and eggs, so two pieces were almost enough for a meal. I needed these supplies, as neither the ship's dishes nor its food were kosher, with the exception of the bread, which was baked directly on stone rather than in a baking dish.

A Jewish woman with two daughters, Sophie and Hope, embarked at Fremantle. She was originally from Rosh Pinna in Israel and was returning to Israel. We became quite friendly and I would join them for afternoon tea, drinking tea and eating my fruit and strudel.

The captain was determined to be in London by 1 August, a bank holiday, so he pushed the boat along to be there on time. He was very careful about safety, cautioning children not to lean over the railings. He would say that as he wasn't responsible for bringing them into the world, he certainly did not want to be responsible for them leaving the world!

Although the ship had pitched from side to side as we crossed the Bight, from Fremantle, it began to pitch from front to back, like a rocking horse. Although plenty of others were seasick, this didn't trouble me at all. As we approached the cross currents of Africa, however, it pitched from side to side again, and again, I was seasick, though not for long.

We finally reached Aden on a Saturday and berthed some way from the shore. Being the Sabbath, Jewish law forbids you to get off a ship and into a smaller boat to reach land so I stayed on the boat. The other Jewish people who disembarked during the day came back with their tails between their legs, as most of the shops were owned by orthodox Jewish people and were closed! After sunset I decided to disembark and as the port was some way from the city of Aden, I asked some others to share a taxi with me. After we had looked around, I then asked the taxi driver to take us to the Jewish quarter. He took us to the synagogue, where the congregants were sitting and wailing. The building was wrecked and we discovered that the Jewish community had been attacked. One of the congregants took us to his home. The family was poor, but they were hospitable, giving us some refreshments and water. That water, from the Queen of Sheba well, was the vilest I had ever tasted!

When we returned to the boat, I noticed a young man who was very sunburnt. His name was Morris Galp and he became the life of the party. I suspected he might be Jewish and tried to get close to him, but he avoided me no matter how hard I tried. One day I cornered him and asked him where he was from. He told me he came from Johannesburg, South Africa, where I said I had an uncle. When he asked my uncle's name I replied, '*Shema Yisroel*.' Immediately he warmed to me and told me he was a stowaway. He had been a pilot in the South

African air force and was going to Israel in answer to a call to Jewish pilots from the fledgling Israeli Government in the lead-up to independence, when trouble was expected. He had worked his way from South Africa to Aden, where he had boarded our ship. The captain had announced that he knew there were stowaways on board, threatening they would be put in irons as soon as they were found.

Galp had not eaten for two days as he wanted to stay out of view of the crew. I had made friends with one of the stewardesses, who had shown me where to find tea, sugar and boiling water, so I told him to come to my cabin when everyone else was having afternoon tea. I gave him tea and something to eat, but two of the others who shared the cabin came in while we were there and accused me of breaking our agreement not to bring strangers in. I managed to get away with convincing them that Galp was a friend for whom I could vouch.

Galp and the others who were going to Israel had to disembark at El Qantara, half way along the Suez Canal, to make their way through Egypt. I asked Galp how he was going to get off and he just told me to wait and see! When we stopped at El Qantara, I stood at the railings watching the Arab coolies unloading to luggage and there was Galp, carting luggage too, very sunburnt and looking exactly like all the others. He gave a wave with his arm to acknowledge me and off he went. I found out later from my friend with the two daughters, who sent a letter for me to Gibraltar (the ship's next port of call), that some Arabs had attacked the train from El Qantara, but nobody had been hurt.

Galp had given me the name of his aunt in Johannesburg, so I wrote to her some years later to find out what had happened to him. As she replied that she didn't know anything about him, I began to doubt the story he had told me. However, many years later, the daughter of friends of ours married a South African. When we made *sheva broches,* I told the groom's father about Galp and he promised to try to find out about him. Sure enough, three weeks later I received a letter with Galp's address. He had returned to South Africa, had married and was living in Capetown. I phoned him and spoke with him and we kept in touch for some time.

It was *Tisha Ba'av* when we passed through the Suez Canal and I was fasting. As there was daylight saving, with the clock two hours ahead of standard time, it was a long day for me. I was very weak by the time sunset came and I thought I would faint if I went to the cabin, so I stayed on deck. There was a dance in progress and drinks were being served, so I ordered a brandy, which helped enough for me to be able to return to the cabin and have something to eat.

After picking up the mail in Gibraltar, the ship headed for London. It had been an exciting journey for a young man who had grown up in Shepparton and hadn't ventured further than Melbourne. Apart from travelling across thousands of kilometres through exotic locations, life on board was made more interesting by the presence of so many different people, some of whom were war brides. These women had married Englishmen in Australia and were going to London to join their husbands. For an unmarried, orthodox Jewish young man, all I can say is that they were as persistent as flies on a humid day!

Apart from their unsolicited attention, these war brides also beat me to the limited food I could eat in the ship's dining room. Having been taught that it was 'ladies before gentlemen', there was little I could do! Altogether, I didn't have too much to eat during the trip and lived on strudel, fruit, bread and tea, and occasionally potatoes which a Jewish waiter cooked for me.

As we approached London, the ship's canteen was opened and passengers were able to buy whatever was available, so I bought a box of sweetened condensed milk and boxes of preserved apricots, peaches and pears. When we docked I had my purchases delivered to my lodgings. They turned out to be very useful as there was rationing in London and food was scarce. If I was invited anywhere, I would take a string bag of these goodies and they were much appreciated.

A porter took my luggage off the ship and helped me find a taxi. The taxi couldn't get to me quickly enough when he heard the porter yell, 'He's right', realising that he too would get a good tip. He delivered me safely to my lodgings, but I was very weak from not eating properly during the voyage and developed boils during my first week in London. With rest and proper food, however, I soon recuperated and was able to begin enjoying life in a new city.

A short time later, I decided to go to a Hachshara camp for Jewish young people in Thackstead, about forty kilometres from London. (Hachshara provided agricultural training to young people intending to migrate to Palestine – later Israel.) They were picking peas and other vegetables and wanted me to work, so I helped them. As they could see I knew about farming, they wanted me to work more, so I agreed to work for half a day if I could have the rest of the day to myself. I spent an enjoyable fortnight there, meeting the young men and women who were on their way to Israel.

On the farm at Thackstead they were using a beautiful chestnut horse to bring the wheat sheaves in from the fields for threshing. There were many drainage channels through the fields and the horse refused to cross the bridges over these channels, making each trip at least three times longer. When they agreed to let me help, I cut a long, thin branch and took the horse for a walk around the field. Every time I steered him to the right or left, I gave him a few good wacks and he soon knew I meant business. I then steered him to a bridge across the channel and made sure he knew I was there. He crossed the bridge without any trouble and after that, there were no further problems and the work took considerably less time.

Back in London I became friendly with another boarder at the Wechslers, who was a *shochet* from Glasgow. He told me about a Jewish man in Blackpool who had a collection of museum pieces that sounded interesting. These pieces were on display before they were packed up to be taken to New York and as there was a kosher hotel in Blackpool, we decided to go and visit.

There were eight or ten of us at the Friday night table – Americans and English – all very friendly and enjoying ourselves singing *zmires*. The next day we went to *shul* and then returned to London on the Sunday. Some fifty years later I discovered that two sisters who had been at that Friday night dinner had come to Sydney, married and set up home there. How did I find out? My granddaughter, who was living in Sydney, became engaged to a Sydney boy and my daughter made an engagement party for them in Melbourne. There I was introduced to the guests from Sydney, including the groom's grandmother. As I was wishing her *mazel tov*, she said, 'I remember you. You're the tall Australian who came to Blackpool and we met at the hotel at that lovely Friday night dinner!'

About two weeks after coming back from Thaxtead I went

by ship to Sweden. I was not only interested in visiting the factory where our saw-mill machinery was made, but I also wanted to see this country which had helped so many Jewish people during and after World War II. I left London on the *Swissea* on 2 September 1947 and was away for two months.

As I was standing on the deck waiting for the ship to leave London, a fellow came up to me. He was wearing a pinstriped suit and bowler hat and was carrying a briefcase, the epitome of an English gentleman. When he told me he was an engineer who was going to work in Sweden, I thought it strange that he was leaving, when postwar Britain was desperate for engineers. He walked away, but when he came up on the other side of me, I realised why he was leaving – his body odour was foul! Trying to get away from him as quickly as I could, I made an excuse to go to my cabin. The cabin just happened to have two berths and who was my roommate to be? It was just my luck that it was my friend in the bowler hat! I was unable to sleep, so I moved my pillow to the other end of my bed facing the door and spent the night leaning out the door with my head in the corridor. Luckily the trip only took three days and two nights!

Before I left London, someone warned me that I would need help finding my way around in Sweden as I didn't speak Swedish. He suggested I find a young female student to help me and told me to introduce myself with the words *'Jag äslkar dig'*. Arriving at the port of Gothenburg, I needed to find the station so I could take a train to Stockholm. I had a small gold map of Australia in my lapel and the Australian chargé d'affaires at the port saw it and invited me home to his place. Being a country boy I was a bit shy and declined the invitation. My primary concern was to find the station, so when I saw a young lady approaching me, I went up to her and said, 'Excuse me, *jag äslkar dig.*' She looked at me, smiled and asked me if I knew what I was saying. I said I didn't but was told to introduce myself that way. It happened to mean 'I love you'! She was a student who had a day off and she offered to show me around. She was a charming girl who took me via the canals to the synagogue and then to see a movie. Before leaving, she showed me how to get to the station and I caught the sleeper train to Stockholm – a beautiful train, much cleaner than the ship from London.

I spent my first night in Stockholm at a hotel, but the next day I went to the Jewish centre and was given the name of some refugee homes which provided accommodation. I chose an orthodox one in the suburb of Ronninge, about half an hour out of the city. All went well until I ran out of foreign currency, which was then in short supply, so I had to live on a very tight budget until my father managed to send me twenty-five pounds ($50).

I stayed in Ronninge for a number of weeks and visited the factory where our machinery was made. I was driven there by a company representative, who told me the factory was eighty miles (one hundred and twenty-eight kilometres) out of Stockholm. When the factory seemed a lot further away than I had anticipated, my host told me that a Swedish mile is the equivalent of four English miles! Finally he asked if I would like to drive, which I did. At that time driving was on the left side of the road in Sweden, so it felt familiar. The drive went smoothly apart from the lucky escape I had when passing an approaching car on a narrow bridge with only a couple of centimetres between us. My companion must have been impressed as he complimented me on my driving skills.

We stayed away overnight and that night for dinner there was moose on the menu, a very special dish in Sweden. My host insisted that I have it, but as the meat was not kosher, I declined, telling him I was a vegetarian. As we were eating, my friend pointed out that the waitresses were Jewish. They were concentration camp survivors, some of the many the Swedish Government had brought to Sweden to look after and restore their health. My host was impressed with their shapeliness and olive skin, which was such a contrast to the Swedes, who were generally tall, thin and blonde.

Back in Stockholm, I had been out one night and was waiting for the train to go back to Ronninge. The weather was freezing cold and the wind was a little lazy – going right through you instead of around you! I was huddled in the corner of the station, not feeling all that well, with a slight temperature. I fell asleep and dreamt that my brothers Dave and Abraham were out in Pine Lodge, a settlement near Shepparton, with Roy Thomas, one of our employees. As I mentioned earlier, a horse, if it gets out, will return to where it was born and one of our horses came from Yabba, a little northeast of Pine Lodge. In my dream, Dave, Abraham and Roy had gone out to bring back some horses which had strayed and they were at the Five Ways intersection, heading the horses back to Shepparton.

I thought nothing more of my dream until I spoke to Dave on the telephone and he asked me if I had been in some kind of windy shed, feeling unwell and dozing. I answered yes and asked if he, Abraham and Roy had been chasing horses on to the Shepparton road, past the church at the Five Ways intersection. We worked out our times and it had happened exactly as I had dreamt it! Years later, in Shepparton, when the fruit was being packed to go to the markets, I would go to phone Dave, who was responsible for marketing the fruit. Just as I was about to pick up the phone, Dave would phone with the information I needed. This kind of telepathy happened between the two of us on several occasions.

I enjoyed my stay in Sweden, especially the opportunity to meet people from other parts of the world. Having Yiddish as a common language was an added bonus in the Jewish community. At a Saturday night get-together in Stockholm, we found that no two people could converse in a common language with the exception of a Canadian and me, the only English speakers. Otherwise, there was a Czech, a Hungarian, a German, a Pole, and other nationalities as well, but we could communicate easily in Yiddish.

The stowaway, Morris Galp

Ruth

On my second Saturday in London, when I had recuperated from my journey from Melbourne, I went to *shul*. After the service a man came up to me, introduced himself as Mr Deutsch and asked me where I was from. When I told him I came from a town near Melbourne in Australia, he asked me if I knew Mr Moshe Feiglin. He was one of the Dunera boys, and when he found out I was Moshe Feiglin's son, he immediately invited me home for lunch.

As Mr Deutsch and I were approaching his home, a young lady and a little girl were coming towards us. I was sure the little girl was Mr Deutsch's daughter, but who was the young lady? Mr Deutsch didn't introduce us, but I wondered if she could be his wife. However, Mr Deutsch introduced me to his wife as soon as we arrived at their home and she then introduced me to the young lady I had seen in the street. Her name was Ruth and Mrs Deutsch told me her story.

Ruth was born in Poland, on the German border, and had escaped with her family to Russia when the German tanks rolled in to Zywiec in 1939. After the war, Ruth's parents were in a displaced persons camp and her brother had remained in Lvov to study medicine. Ruth's young cousin Shulamit had spent the war years in hiding in the house of a peasant family. Her health was poor, so her father, Ruth's Uncle Mendel, decided she would have a better chance of recovering in England. As she was unable to travel alone and fend for herself, he asked Ruth's parents if she could accompany Shulamit to London.

Ruth and Shulamit had come to London with Rabbi Schoenfeld and a group of Jewish children. The rabbi had arranged for Jewish families to take them into their homes and that was how Ruth and Shulamit came to be living with the Deutsches. As permits to enter the United Kingdom were not available for children over sixteen and the rabbi had told his charges not to divulge their ages, everyone assumed Ruth was sixteen.

At this time the Deutsches had one daughter and Mrs Deutsch was pregnant with their second child. As she was concerned about who would look after her daughter while she was in hospital, she asked Ruth to help. Ruth cared for the child and the house and when Mrs Deutsch came home from hospital she was most surprised. She was expecting to see the house in a mess and the child untidy, but the house was spick and span and the child could not have been cleaner or happier. Mrs Deutsch hugged Ruth, saying, 'For this I will take you to the *chuppah*.'

After I met Ruth we continued to see each other at the Deutsches, go for walks together and enjoy each other's company. Ruth had a girlfriend with whom she spent a lot of time and I would often bump into them when they were out walking. And so the relationship grew. Mrs Deutsch saw this and one day asked me if I was interested in marrying Ruth. I replied that I did not think it was a good idea as I was twenty-six and she was only sixteen, but somehow, in my heart, I felt that something may develop.

I continued to meet other young people and made new friends, including two girls and a young man I met while watching a parade of Jewish troops through the streets of London.

A few months later, Mrs Deutsch telephoned to tell me to come over to her place. I was ten minutes' brisk walk away, but I was having breakfast and told her I would come when I was finished. She insisted that it was important and I should come immediately, so I did. As soon as I arrived, Mrs Deutsch told me she had just found out that Ruth was nineteen, not sixteen. Ruth had explained that she had had to conceal her age to obtain a permit to enter the United Kingdom, and also so that she could attend school.

Although we had already spent quite a lot of time together, we began to go out alone. I can still remember seeing the movie *I Wonder Who's Kissing Her Now* together! Three weeks later I proposed and Ruth accepted.

Just before our official engagement, Ruth wrote to her parents, who were then living in Milan, telling them that she was soon to marry an Australian. Her father wrote back to her, asking how she knew if her fiancé was Jewish, and confirming that he was white! Her parents even made a special trip to the Australian Embassy in Rome to find out the name of an orthodox rabbi in Melbourne who could tell them something about my background.

Ruth's father then wrote to Rabbi Gurewitz in Melbourne, as well as to my father. My father not only wrote back, but also sent a photo of himself and my mother with one of their grandchildren. Rabbi Gurewitz also replied and what Ruth's father read must have reassured him. My parents were fortunate to have a little more information about Ruth because Mr Liebler, a friend of my brother's from Melbourne, was in

London, so we arranged to visit him. He was very impressed with Ruth and phoned my brother, who passed his impressions on to my parents.

I telephoned my parents to tell them about our engagement. Long distance calls had to be connected by an operator, and when the operator rang the person who was to receive the call, all the other phones connected to the same exchange rang too. So, the news of our engagement was heard by anyone in Shepparton who cared to listen to my conversation with my parents!

Five weeks later we were married and were on the ship to Australia. Before the wedding, however, I went on a short trip to Paris. Ruth's Uncle Mendel had been living in Paris and as soon as we were engaged, Ruth wrote to him to tell him she would not be able to look after Shulamit when we were married. As a result, her uncle came to London. He had been planning to take Shulamit to Chile anyway and was half packed, but still had things in his apartment and in customs. He had planned to come back to Paris with his daughter before going to Chile, but the French Government decided otherwise. As Poland by then had a Communist government and the French Government forbade entry into France to anyone with a passport from a Communist country, Uncle Mendel's Polish passport would not allow him back to Paris. As I could easily come and go with my Australian passport, he asked me to go and finish packing up his apartment and clear the rest of his goods through customs.

As I could not refuse, I booked a ticket on the second flight out of London the following Sunday morning. I was unable to sleep on Saturday night and felt as if there was an angel shaking me, to keep me awake. Instead of tossing and turning in bed, I got up very early and went to the airport to check in, arriving half an hour before the first flight was due to depart. As there were plenty of available seats, the airline attendant suggested I go on that flight, so I did.

Ruth had asked me to send her a telegram when I arrived in Paris but the post office was closed on a Sunday and I was told a postcard would be just as quick. I sent the card, bought some bread and found Uncle Mendel's apartment. There I met a friend of his whom he had asked to help me so that I could organise this business as quickly as possible. She was a young woman from Germany in her late twenties, an Auschwitz survivor.

This young lady sat on the end of the bed while I took a tin of kosher meat I had brought from Australia, boiled it up in the tin and opened it on to the only plate in the apartment. I gave her a fork and used my knife to divide our food in half. She refused to eat, claiming she was not hungry, but I did not believe her. As she kept on insisting, I said in my best Yiddish-German that if she didn't share the meal, I would throw it out. This she could not stand, so we both tucked in and enjoyed our meal.

The next morning I arranged to go to the customs offices to clear Mendel's belongings. Mendel had given me instructions not to let anyone open his big, wooden crate, but of course customs officer wanted to see what was inside. Despite my protests, he insisted. After opening it, he scratched around one corner and then the other, closing the crate without another word. To this day, I do not know what was in it!

After clearing customs I went back to the apartment and began packing according to Mendel's instructions. He had told me where to find two American five-hundred-dollar bills, which I concealed in the cover of the book I was reading. He also had a diamond ring, two gold bracelets and two watches, as well as a heavy suitcase full of new linen. I put on the wristwatch and hid the rest of the jewellery in my clothes. I presumed perhaps I was doing something illegal, so I took every precaution to cover myself. I then took all Mendel's belongings to the port and took the boat back to London.

After disembarking at Tilbury Docks, I had to deal with customs officials again. An Australian rugby team had been in Paris, so we chatted about rugby – about which I knew nothing – but the customs officer finally wanted to check my things. There had been a lot of smuggling of wristwatches, so when he saw the watch on my wrist he cross-examined me so closely I thought I would end up in the Old Bailey! I was so worried that my arm began to shake and I remarked that I had hurt my shoulder playing rugby. I had never played in my life, but he swallowed my story. He eventually realised I was no smuggler and let me go.

I was the last one out of customs, and when I finally emerged, there was Uncle Mendel with a long, drawn face. Ruth was standing behind him, as white as a ghost and shaking like a leaf. When I asked Ruth what was the matter, she told me that the flight on which I had originally been booked had crashed on landing in Paris and had caught fire. There had been no survivors. Obviously, my postcard had not arrived! I had seen a burnt-out plane on the tarmac when I went to clear Mendel's goods through customs, but it hadn't entered my head that it could be the plane on which I had originally been booked.

Back in London, we were busy with wedding preparations, although there was not much I had to do. I had a suit, and the

Deutsches looked care of everything else, true to their promise to Ruth to take her to the *chuppah.*

Our wedding took place at Greenlanes Synagogue on 11 January 1948, followed by a reception at Kedassia kosher restaurant in the city. Our guests included Uncle Mendel and Shulamit, the only family we had in London, and two other Australians – Rabbi Brodie from Melbourne and Abe Yoffee.

I had a ticket to go back to Melbourne by ship, but I knew it would be very difficult to buy a ticket for Ruth, so I went to Burns Phillips, the shipping line, to see what I could do. The response was that if I wanted to take my wife with me I would have to wait three years! I returned a couple of days later and explained that I wanted to take my wife back to Melbourne to meet my mother, who was terminally ill, offering the official some new pound notes to help him with the expenses. Two days later I had the ticket!

Our trip from London to Melbourne on the *Strathaird* should have taken four weeks but as we approached Bombay, one of the ship's motors blew up. Engineers were flown out from London and they decided the ship would be able to carry on with two motors instead of three, delaying our arrival by a week.

As my niece was getting married in Melbourne, we disembarked in Adelaide and flew to Melbourne to arrive in time for the wedding. Ruth's reputation as a beautiful person – inside and out – had preceded us, and the whole family was very excited to meet her. As soon as the *simcha* was over, Ruth and I left Melbourne with my brother and his family, arriving in Shepparton at dawn the next morning.

Aaron (centre) being taken to the chuppah with Abe Yoffee,
Henry Deutsch, Mr Lublin and Ruth's uncle, Mendel Kanarek,
London, 1948

Ruth and Aaron's marriage, with Ruth's cousin, Shulamit, Ruth's
Uncle Mendel, Tony Lublin and Abe Yoffee

Ruth and Aaron's wedding, 1948

Ruth and Aaron with Mr and Mrs Deutsch, London, 1974

Ruth and Aaron in Port Said, on the way back to Australia, 1948

The next generation

When Ruth and I first came to Shepparton, we stayed with my parents for several months until our own home was ready. Sam had married a couple of months earlier, so all my brothers and sisters had left home. My parents had built a new home in 1941, and an old house had also been shifted to our property. Half of this house was being used to house workers further up the road and the other half was next door to my parents' home. A kitchen was being added to the two bedrooms and this cottage was where we were to make our first home.

Living with parents can sometimes be problematic, but in our case, nothing could have been further from reality. From the beginning, my parents treated Ruth like a beloved daughter and they all enjoyed each other's company. Ruth and my mother spent many hours talking and exchanging experiences. By this stage, my mother was not very well and Ruth helped with the cooking and anything else which would help lighten the burden for my mother.

One day my mother drew me aside and quietly and earnestly told me that my wife was a *berieh*, which in translation means a person capable in any field in which she is put. Of course I had also come to that conclusion much, much earlier!

As soon as the cottage was ready, we moved in. We had

breakfast and lunch there, but Ruth would prepare our main meal and we would eat with my parents in the evening, as we did every Friday night and Saturday. For the third meal of the Sabbath, we were joined by my sister and brother-in-law and their children, and we all enjoyed singing the *zmires* together.

As soon as we had settled into the cottage, we turned our thoughts to bringing Ruth's parents out to Australia. These were troubled times in Europe: the Cold War had begun and the Soviet blockade on all land and water communication between West Berlin and West Germany was in force. Ruth's parents were in a displaced persons camp in Italy and my family advised us to send them the money for air fares so that they could join us. Unfortunately the three and a half thousand pounds ($7000) was mostly swallowed up by the organisations involved in arranging the travel for the thousands of people trying to leave Europe. Ruth's parents finally arrived in Melbourne by ship in September 1948. They stayed with us for four weeks, but as Ruth's father was unable to find work in Shepparton, they decided to settle in Melbourne.

The year 1949 was a big one for us: I took over the management of the orchards from my brother Abraham, who moved to Melbourne, and Ruth was pregnant with our first child. My mother would not hear of 'her' Ruth having the baby in Shepparton and insisted she go to a top specialist, so Ruth moved to Melbourne for the last month of her pregnancy and stayed with her parents.

By then, my mother was very ill and had also moved to Melbourne so that her daughters could look after her. On one occasion when Ruth and I were visiting her, Mother called us in to her room and told us we would have a girl. She asked that we call her Leah, so that when we went back to Shepparton she would be with us in spirit as well as name.

Our first child, a daughter, was born in Melbourne on 12 December 1949. Even though my mother had requested we name the baby after her, I was still in a quandary about what to do, as Jewish tradition does not permit the naming of a child after a living parent. I went to see Rabbi Wilshansky, whose advice was that as it was my mother's wish, and in view of her condition, we should obey her. So it was that our first-born child was named Leah.

Sadly, my mother passed away only ten days after Leah's birth, so we stayed in Melbourne for *shiva* before returning to Shepparton.

Our second child, Yitzchok, was born in 1952. That was also the year my sister Bertha moved to Melbourne, so we were able to move into her three-bedroom house next door to my parents place, which was much roomier than the cottage.

Following the birth of Leah and Yitzchok, we were blessed with three more children. Amira was born in 1953, but as Yitzchok could not pronounce her name, he called her Mimi, the name she has been called ever since. Avigdor was born in 1956 and Naomi in 1961.

As our two older children approached school age, we had to decide what kind of education we wanted them to have. The choice was between government and Jewish schools, but attending Jewish schools would require us to set up house in Melbourne. After much discussion, Ruth and I agreed that giving the children a Jewish education was our first priority, so we made plans to move the family to Melbourne.

We came to East St Kilda in 1953 and Ruth enrolled Leah at

kindergarten. At that stage there were no Jewish kindergartens in the area, so Leah went to Miss Miller's in Inkerman Road. All went well until the end of the year, when we found Leah sitting up in bed at night singing Christmas carols. Ruth was not at all happy, so she contacted the other Jewish mothers she knew in the local area and suggested they start their own kindergarten. As a result, the first Jewish kindergarten in Caulfield was established at the Caulfield *shul*.

By the time Leah finished kindergarten, Mount Scopus Memorial College had been established in St Kilda Road, so Leah went to school there. In 1954, the Yeshivah Centre established the Yeshivah College for boys in East St Kilda, so Yitzchok and Avigdor went to school there. Five years later, the Yeshivah Centre established Beth Rivkah College for girls and Leah moved there from Mount Scopus. Both Mimi and Naomi also went to Beth Rivkah. My father, through his close relationship with the Lubbavitcher Rebbe in New York, had been instrumental in the establishment of both Yeshivah and Beth Rivkah Colleges, so our children were able to reap the benefits of his work.

When we moved to Melbourne, I commuted to the orchards during the week. During winter I would spend two or three nights a week in Shepparton, but during the ten weeks or so of harvest I was away for five, and occasionally six, nights a week. Most weeks I would arrive in Melbourne on Thursday night and return to Shepparton on Monday.

Father had moved to Melbourne in 1952 and was living in a house in Balaclava Road, East St Kilda, and we stayed with him for a few months until we bought and renovated our house at 515 Inkerman Road. He would mostly come with me to Shepparton. Ruth would cook for us and we would set off with her food and a supply of meat and vegetables.

My routine at Shepparton was to get up, *daven*, go out to allocate jobs to the workers and then come inside to have breakfast. My father would always rise from bed before daybreak, have a session of biblical studies, recite his psalms, then *daven* and be finished in time to join me for breakfast.

April 1957 was a particularly hot month and one day I came inside to find my father sitting in his armchair, not yet having had his usual hot drink. I offered to make him a cup of tea and when he refused, I immediately guessed that he was fasting. When I asked him why, he tried to push my question aside, but I persisted in asking. He finally said that the previous night he had dreamt that 'his time was up'. I left it at that but insisted he have a drink after two in the afternoon.

A week after *Pesach*, which was about three weeks later, he was knocked over by a car as he was walking home from *shul*. The young female driver had looked back to wave to her friend, so she had not seen him. He rolled in front of the car and was badly bruised, but he managed to get back home and notify the carer who lived in a unit behind his house. She called an ambulance and he was taken to hospital.

I visited Father daily and on Friday I stayed with him for as long as I could. He sat up and told me to go before the Sabbath commenced. I was the last member of the family to see him alive. He passed away the next morning, 4 May 1957.

The funeral procession went from his home in East St Kilda to the Carlton cemetery and was so large that the police had to be called to direct the traffic. The funeral itself was officiated by Rabbi Abramson (a Lubavitcher rabbi from Sydney who was related to our family). Although he spoke with deep feeling and sincerity, I was oblivious to it all as I was heartbroken beyond imagination. I had lived and travelled with my father for such a long time and suddenly this was broken off. It took me a long time to come to terms with his loss.

* * *

I had always wanted to build a house and the opportunity arose quite unexpectedly. One Sunday morning I was walking past the dilapidated house two doors from our place and the old widow who lived there was sitting on the front veranda, crying her eyes out. When I asked her what the matter was, she told me she was living there all alone and wanted to sell the house. I asked the price and she told me four thousand five hundred pounds ($8000), a large amount of money in those days. I immediately phoned my brother Dave, an estate agent, who advised me what to do and I ended up buying the house. The house took around nine months to build and we moved to 519 Inkerman Road in 1967.

Back in Shepparton, it was nerve-wracking to make sure that all work was done in the autumn, winter and spring; to have the crop on the trees and to be able to bring it to the market place. Added to this was my situation of commuting backwards and forwards to Melbourne, which left me drained of energy, particularly during the summer months.

To get back to Melbourne on Friday afternoon before Shabbat, I would have to plan precisely the time I would need. When I left Shepparton, I would usually drive for about fifteen minutes and be overtaken by fatigue. I would stop at a shady spot about twenty-five kilometres from Shepparton, where I would set my little timer and have a nap. One Friday, after a particularly trying week, I managed to get within seven kilometres of my usual stop, but I was so tired, I fell asleep while driving. I was awakened by a semitrailer coming towards me and saw that I was almost on a narrow bridge that crossed a deep creek.

That episode frightened me out of my wits, so I would sing as loudly as I could until I reached my resting place. A nap of twenty to thirty minutes was sufficient for me to get home.

By this stage, all my brothers were involved in the timber mills and I was the only one involved in the orchards. We had meetings every Thursday night initially, but these later became fortnightly before stopping altogether after my father passed away. From then on, we discussed business matters by phone and although nothing was ever put in writing, we had no problems in reaching decisions.

Ruth and the children always came to Shepparton for the school holidays. The children would wrap up their bedding, put it in plastic bags and throw it in the big trailer I had built. They loved their holidays on the orchards and, as we approached Shepparton, they would start singing their special song which went something like 'We're nearly there, we're nearly at Shepparton!'

I bought a 1926 model Chevrolet car and the children all learnt to drive at an early age. Avigdor learnt to drive when he was about twelve and one time, when his cousin came to stay with us, Avigdor let him drive. He released the clutch suddenly so that the differential gave way, but we just happened to have a spare differential from a wrecked car of the same model. Under the guidance of the mechanic on the property, Avigdor was able to pull it out and fix the car. All seemed under control until he tried to drive the car and, lo and behold, he had three reverse gears and only one forward gear! Glued to the radio as he was working on the car, Avigdor had the misfortune to hear that his best friend, Julian Levy, had drowned in Lake Epilock while at a Bnei Akiva camp. Eventually he managed to fix the car.

The children loved swimming and Ruth would take them to the lake and supervise them, even though she could not swim. One day Avigdor went missing and fearing he had gone into the water, Ruth ran to the lifesavers, who blew their whistles. Everyone immediately came out of the water and the children all lined up, but Avigdor was nowhere to be seen. Eventually he appeared from around the corner. He had not been in the water, but had been collecting bottles so that he could make enough money to buy a third icy-pole!

We used to take the children to the Keysties Bridge on the Broken River, where I built a 'dressing shed' for them – old manure bags attached to four trees. One day, when Avigdor was twelve, I took him swimming and as he was coming back towards me, there was the largest tiger snake I have ever seen. Tiger snakes have distinct stripes and their venom is extremely poisonous. I called out to Avigdor to stand still, which he did, and the snake slithered away from us through the grass. Otherwise it was a lovely spot and we all enjoyed swimming there.

Ruth and Aaron in Shepparton, 1968

Ruth and Leah, the first grandchild to be named after Aaron's late
mother, Shepparton, 1950

Managing the orchards

When I took over the management of the orchards, I was familiar with every aspect of the work and enjoyed the challenge of taking on more responsibility and putting new innovations into practice. This involved not just the Shepparton property, but Cobram as well, which I would visit once a week, or more when it was necessary.

At Shepparton we had forty-nine hectares of orchards with two hundred and fifty trees per hectare. At Cobram we had eighty-five hectares, with fewer trees per acre because the ground was more fertile than in Shepparton. As a result, the trees were planted further apart so that they grew larger and yielded more fruit.

At first we mainly grew Williams Bon Crétien (known as WBC) pears, as these were the only kind used for canning. The cannery specified the size of pears they needed and if they were too large, they went to the cannery at Mooroopna for making juice. We also grew Packham, Buerre Bosc, Winter Nelis and Josephine pears, eating pears which were harvested at different times. We grew peaches as well as pears for the cannery. Initially we would have to sort them for size and markings, but in later years, the cannery took over the sorting by machine. The rejected peaches were used for juice, both for drinking and to go in the cans of fruit.

At Cobram we planted peaches first but in later years, when the peach trees became too old to yield profitable crops, we replaced them with pear trees. Because of the fertile soil in Cobram, we were able to get the pears to a marketable size much earlier and sell them to the domestic market.

Every season had its jobs to do, but harvest time was the busiest time of the year. We had three or four people working permanently in the orchards on each property, but during the summer harvest we would employ almost anyone who was prepared to pick fruit. This could mean twenty or thirty extra people at Shepparton and a similar number at Cobram over a period of several weeks.

Some of the fruit pickers lived in Shepparton, whilst others came from other parts of Victoria or from interstate. We were able to house ten or twelve in the huts on our property and the others brought tents or caravans. Many were itinerant workers, some were students and, later, backpackers. In the days when sugar cane was cut by hand, the cane cutters were strong men used to hot summers, who would finish cutting the cane in Queensland in time to come down south to pick fruit. We lost this source of labour when mechanisation of the sugar cane harvest became more widespread in the 1960s and cane cutters found alterative employment.

One year, a fruit picker came along who did nothing but stir up trouble. He was an Irishman who didn't want to work and he was an impossible influence on the other workers. I tried to send him away, but he wouldn't go, so I finally called the police to get rid of him. Another time we had two workers – one Hungarian and one Pole – who argued. The Hungarian suggested they shake hands, presumably to make peace, but he grabbed the Pole's hand and broke it across his knee! Otherwise, we had very few problems with the fruit pickers.

Other orchardists would work seven days a week during the harvest, but of course we would never work on Saturdays, so our workers also enjoyed our Sabbath break. To this day they still regret not working for us!

Once the fruit was picked, it would go to a large shed to be sorted for the cannery and graded and packed for the fresh fruit market. The huge fruit sorter was on one side of the shed and the grader on the other side. The sorter was capable of handling two to three tonnes of pears per hour and was used by the workers to manually remove the second-quality fruit. The grader sorted fruit mechanically to size before being packing into cartons and sent to the market.

Angelina, the wife of my right-hand man, Angelo, used to operate these machines, a job she did diligently and capably, so much so that I became completely reliant on her. We were used to everything going smoothly, but one day, one of the workers caught his jumper on a protruding bolt on a moving shaft of the grader. Although it was only a minor accident, a saying by King Solomon immediately came to mind: Who is a wise person the one who can foresee what can happen. I summoned the electrician and asked him to put stop buttons wherever necessary for the workers to be able to stop the machine easily in an emergency.

Some time after, I was leaning over the grader cleaning a belt that had jammed when a strand of wool from my cardigan caught on the bolt. I began to be dragged into the machine and screamed out to whoever was nearby to stop it. Angelina immediately pounced on the stop button and a serious accident was avoided. A large wrench spanner had to be used to wind the machine back to release me, but otherwise I was unhurt.

One of the first things I was able to do when I took over as manager of the orchards was begin using a hormone spray which saved an enormous amount of fruit. Where the stalk of the pear joins the tree branch, it is very vulnerable to movement, so the fruit can easily fall. The spray – with the brand name Stick-On – encouraged a very fine skin to grow at this point, allowing the fruit to move in the wind, but preventing it from falling to the ground.

At this time DDT (Dichlorodiphenyltrichloroethane), which was used to spray against codlin moth, came on to the market for the first time. The Shepparton Fruit Growers Association obtained a small quantity and as I was friendly with the president, he offered it to me first. He had six or eight drums, which I immediately accepted, even though it was very expensive. Although my brother was not very happy about the cost, my father supported me, as he believed you should always honour an agreement, even a verbal one.

About eighty percent of our fruit was grown for the canneries in Shepparton and the rest was sold to the markets. If the cannery found codlin moth in our pears, they would either be rejected or the price would be reduced. As a result, we had a line of workers inspecting every one of our pears before they left for the cannery. Each pear was taken out of its box and its calyx (tail), stem and, lastly, the fruit's surface, were inspected. Often evidence of codlin moth was very hard to see at first, but it developed into something much more obvious by the time it was inspected at the cannery.

When we started spraying with DDT, we found that the

pears showed no sign of codlin moth. As a result, we only inspected for size, shape and unacceptable markings, and the time and labour we saved inspecting the fruit more than made up for the cost of the spray. At that stage no one thought that DDT was harmful, although evidence later indicated that it was and it was banned in Australia in 1987. Fortunately, by then there were other chemicals to replace it.

Some of our spraying was not quite so predictable. I used to grow vegetables on the plot of land next door to our cottage – tomatoes, carrots and beetroot. Mr McArthur, from whom I bought my tomato plants, grew hundreds of thousands of tomatoes to supply the twelve factories in Shepparton that made tomato sauce and juice. One day, Mr McArthur asked me for advice about spraying his pear trees against black spot, a lethal fungus which can affect pear and apple trees during spring. In order to prevent the spores of the fungus from landing on the fruit, the trees are sprayed when they are in bud with a copper spray. No one knew the best time to spray, so we would spray the trees three times, hoping we would be successful at some stage. As Mr McArthur had been so busy with his tomato plants, he had completely missed spraying his trees.

The petals were already falling off the flowers, and Mac, as he was known, was ready to write off his pears. 'Mac, are you telling me, or are you asking me?' I asked, and his reply was that he wanted my opinion. As he had put the effort into irrigating and pruning his trees, I thought it was still worth spraying them. He took my advice and managed to hit the jackpot, while the rest of us, who had sprayed earlier, lost ninety per cent of our fruit. In fact, our crops were so bad that the cannery inspectors advised us to salvage every bit of fruit we could, even if it was only a quarter of a pear.

One day Mr McArthur told me he had sixteen hectares of land on the outskirts of Shepparton which he wanted to sell, as he wanted to buy a dairy farm for his two boys. He had been growing tomatoes there and he wanted me to 'beg, borrow or steal' in order to buy it. It would have been a very good investment, but foolishly, I did nothing about it.

The fruit we grew for the markets was transported by semitrailer to Sydney and Melbourne. Our orchards had very good soil and were well managed, so we had a lot of early-harvest pears. We were able to get these to the Sydney market before other growers. As Sydney was a big market, we did very well as a result.

We sent pears to Sydney when they were green and they would ripen naturally in the humid climate. It was different in Melbourne, however, where fruiterers had to store the pears on shelves for two weeks to ripen. I had read somewhere that bananas and tomatoes were ripened with the help of ethylene (a gas), so I decided to try it with pears. At this stage we were already growing more pears at Cobram than peaches, and those pears grew to the right size and maturity much sooner than the pears at Shepparton. As a result, we would pick the pears at Cobram, transport them to Shepparton and treat them with ethylene, then send them to Melbourne, where we had our own stand at the wholesale fruit market. There was always a mad scramble by buyers, as our pears were not only ready to eat, but they were the first available pears of the season.

I decided to experiment with using steam in conjunction with the ethylene to hasten the ripening process. I placed the boxes of pears in large chambers, with tubes coming through the ceiling attached to cylinders of ethylene, and had urns of water with heat-immersers inside them to heat the water and provide the steam to work in conjunction with the gas.

I was not going to share my method of ripening pears with the other growers, but they were anxious to know, so one decided to try to find out in the middle of the night. As it was dark in the shed, he stumbled over one of the urns and was scalded with hot water. Venting his anger, he knocked over the stacks of fruit, making a huge mess.

The next day, he was at the cannery with towels wrapped around his legs. As soon as I saw him I knew he was the culprit and chided him, asking him what had happened. I should have taken him to the police for the damage he had done, but he had not been able to find out my secret and he had not escaped unscathed!

The Shepparton Fruit Growers Association was the organisation representing orchardists in the area and had about seventy members when I was managing our orchards. We all operated independently, but got together regularly to share ideas about developments in agriculture and marketing. It was not till quite a few years later that I told the others about my innovative method of ripening pears.

M Feiglin & Sons made the boxes for the fruit destined for the markets, but the cannery supplied the boxes for the fruit we picked for canning. We would distribute the boxes around the orchards before the harvest, in readiness for the pickers to fill. In autumn, after the harvest, we would collect any unused boxes, as well as any broken tree limbs left lying on the ground.

When the leaves fell off the trees it was time to start pruning. Pruning was a specialised job done by our permanent workers, with five or six others employed to help. Just before the end of the trees' growing season in autumn, we would dress the soil with fertiliser in readiness for their new growing season in spring. In winter, after the pruning was finished, we would cultivate the soil, then in spring we would spray against fungus, insects and grubs and fertilise again, continuing to fertilise during the growing period from spring through to autumn.

I saw many changes during my six decades in the orchards. At first we would spray each tree individually by walking around carrying pressurised pumps with wands attached. Then, in the late 1950s, we would stand on the platform of a pump pulled by a tractor, which speeded up the process. Later, a machine was developed, also pulled by a tractor, which used a fan to push the spray out on to trees on either side of the pump. This further sped up the spraying.

Initially the machines had small fans and were very slow, so I thought it worth experimenting by using a more highly powered motor to drive a larger fan. The manufacturer agreed to contribute the labour if I contributed the materials and we went ahead. He built a new machine using a big fan and a V8 motor. We then invited all the orchardists for a demonstration and it was a resounding success, speeding up the orchardists' work and providing the manufacturer with lots of business. Although today's machines are more sophisticated, they operate on the same principle.

We used to have cultivators which would turn the soil in the orchards to remove the wild grasses which would otherwise eat up the fertiliser. In the 1970s, however, the Department of Agriculture suggested we plant clover and mow it back into the soil as mulch instead. This proved very successful. Pruning methods also changed. Whereas we used to prune the trees, pick up the cuttings and burn them, it was later found that the cuttings could also be put back into the soil. A machine was developed to pulverise the cuttings, which would then rot on the ground, both improving the soil and saving labour and money. The spreading of fertiliser by hand was also eventually taken over by a special machine towed by tractor; not only did it spread the fertiliser on the ground, but you could also set the amount required for each tree.

Shepparton's rainfall averaged around fifty-six centimetres a year and we depended on irrigation to grow our fruit. There was a considerable amount of wastage as water from the drainage channels would flow into the river, but I obtained a permit to pump this water back into the orchards. Although at that stage there seemed to be plenty of water, this water permit proved invaluable in later years as there was often far less rainfall. As we have experienced so many years of drought in recent times, the new owners of our property continue to thank me for it.

In 1956 Shepparton received one hundred and thirty-two centimetres of rain, more than twice the annual average. It made work in the orchards a nightmare and it was impossible to do the winter spraying. The horses could not pull the spray pump and the tractor went down in the soupy soil. It then took us three days to dig it out, even though it was a crawler tractor which could normally handle tough conditions.

As I was standing in the shed with the employees looking

121

at the rain and wondering if we would ever get any of the essential tasks done, I cursed the rain loud and clear. My father, who was standing not very far away, called me over and said, 'Aaron, a blessing from the Almighty you do not curse!' How wise he was and what a help in putting my feelings into perspective!

The good news was that the Eildon Weir had been completed and was ready to receive water, so that all the run off from the floods ended up in the weir. Consequently the weir, which was estimated to take eight or nine years to fill, was full in one year. Had the weir not been functioning, it was said that Shepparton could have been at least three and a half metres under water.

Looking after an orchard involves planting, watering, fertilising, harvesting and pruning. If this sounds complicated enough, it can become much more complicated when you add the element of managing the people involved. For the most part this was not a problem, but in 1989 I had an issue with one of the lads I was teaching to prune, something which was to cost our insurance company dearly.

We would prune the trees in winter when they were dormant. Pruning is a specialist job and incorrect pruning can lose you the following year's crop, as well as that of the year after. That particular year, pruners were hard to find. I had trained two young men two years earlier, one of whom had an Aboriginal mother and a German father. He was accurate, fast and sensible, and both lads were good at their work. I decided to employ two more lads to work alongside these two who had experience and could help the newcomers.

I advertised and employed two more lads and I was happy

with their progress. At that time, there was looper grub about, so I asked Angelo to spray. Being sensible and reliable, Angelo went to the block where the four lads were working and instructed them to go up wind while he was spraying and return only when the trees were dry. One of the late-starter lads was a bit of a smart guy who saw an opportunity and told the others he would 'get a house and a car out of the Feiglins for this'.

In due course we received a summons to appear in court charged with endangering our employee. The case was scheduled for some months later and our insurance company hired a well-known barrister to defend the case. When the barrister came to Shepparton I suggested I sit in on the case, as he did not know anything about spraying fruit trees, but he declined my offer.

The spray we used against looper was Dipel, a product made from vegetable matter that was so harmless that you could bathe in it or even drink it. However, we had also used Parathine to spray against codlin moth a year earlier, when the fruit was on the trees. Parathine happened to be a toxic and vile-smelling chemical.

The spray pump used by the workers to fill their vats and add the chemicals was in an area that was unattended, so anyone could come and go as they wished. Near the spray pump was a heap of twenty-litre drums, stacked and waiting to be taken to the rubbish tip. These drums had been used the previous year to spray Parathine. Although toxic and smelly when mixed with water, the Parathine had dried up in the drums. We were not spraying with Parathine while the boys were pruning and they had no reason to come in contact with the spray material.

During the court case the plaintiff argued that his health had been affected by the spraying. He was asked if he had seen the spray pump being filled and he replied that he had seen the white powder floating everywhere. What he had seen was the Dipel, which, as I have said, was no more than harmless vegetable matter.

As the case developed, the plaintiff's mother gave evidence, proclaiming under oath that every night her son would come home smelling terrible as a result of the spray. I was not there to hear her, but I was told that during her testimony her face was awash with tears. What I believe happened was that she had gone into the orchard when no one else was around, swished some water around in one of the drums of dried-up Parathine and sprinkled it on her son's clothes.

The barrister did not challenge the mother's evidence, even though he knew we had only sprayed the trees once with Dipel while the boys were pruning there. The judge found the company guilty and awarded the worker $500,000 in damages. Later, I found out that he had had nephritis as a child, but this did not come out in the court case. I still wish I had been in the courtroom to state my case. To this day, I'm left with many unanswered questions.

Growing top-quality fruit was essential to being financially successful and this is what I strove to do. However, there were some things that were beyond human control, such as wind storms, which you had to take in your stride and deal with as best you could.

Australia had been exporting large quantities of canned fruit to England, but when the United Kingdom joined the Common Market (later the European Union) in 1973, priority was given to imports from other Common Market countries. As a result, we fruit growers were left stranded. Unable to sell fruit to the cannery, many orchardists cut down their Williams Bon Crétien trees and grafted varieties like Packham that they could sell for eating.

The directors of M Feiglin & Sons initially decided to sit quietly and wait for things to sort themselves out. However, I could see that the future outlook was bleak, so I began by cutting down a small proportion of our trees and grafting the fresh-fruit variety Packham Triumph. Our failure to act quickly cost us dearly, but the company reversed our original decision and we began to graft as many trees as possible to grow the Packham variety.

We still had contracts with SPC, but they were very much reduced and we needed another outlet to sell our fruit. As our fruit had a reputation for high quality, I was approached by an orchardist who supplied the Coles and Safeway supermarket chains. We agreed that he would take the choice fruit suitable to sell to the supermarkets and I would supply the rest to the cannery, and I drew up a small contract to that effect. The orchardist signed the contract in an illegible scrawl, and one of his friends witnessed it, which he did in a similar scrawl.

After we had completed the formalities, I began to supply this orchardist with large quantities of pears. One day, I dropped by to see how things were going. The orchardist was grading his friend's fruit, most of which was unsuitable, before beginning to grade ours, which was of high quality, with ninety percent meeting his requirements.

Some time later, when I came to collect my money, he ripped off a hefty number of dollars from the agreed price. I showed him our contract, but he denied that the scrawl he had made was his signature, leaving me stunned. Needless to say, I decided not to do business with him again, but the next year, he found out that I had a perfect crop of Buerre Bosc pears in a cool store.

As he wanted both the quantity and quality I had in order to fill his order with Safeway, I was able to quote him the highest price possible. The following day I drove the semitrailer to deliver the fruit, arranging with the cool-store owner that I would bring the fruit back if necessary. When I arrived, the orchardist inspected the fruit. I could see he was well satisfied, but I would not let it be unloaded until I had been paid. Realising I did not trust him, he told me he did not want the fruit, so I turned the truck around to drive away, telling him I always stood by any deal I made. Just as I was about to leave, he relented and paid me.

Despite this kind of unpleasant experience, most of the people I dealt with were honourable. The inspector of the cannery, with the respect he showed for my religious beliefs, provides a good example. At the height of the fruit season we were bringing in the crop of pears for delivery to the cannery. It was Friday and I was busy taking load after load to the cannery where the fruit was inspected and weighed. Towards the end of the day, I had a big load to deliver, but I did not think I could have it processed and be back home in time for the Sabbath.

I decided to take a chance. There was a large queue, as all the other orchardists were delivering their fruit as well. I approached the inspector and explained that if I waited in the queue, I would never get home before the Sabbath. As I had exactly the same line of fruit I had previously delivered, I suggested he deduct the same percentage of unusable fruit from this load. As a lad he had worked for my father and he understood the rush to get everything done before sunset. As a result, he dispensed with the usual inspection, signed my book and sent me off immediately to have the fruit weighed and unloaded.

Aaron with his Pakham pears, around 1985

More than apples and pears

When Britain's entry into the Common Market slashed a large part of agricultural incomes, I looked to see what else I could do to provide for my growing family.

As I mentioned earlier, I was always interested in horses and decided to try my hand at horse breeding. Arab horses were in great demand, so I went to Wagga Wagga Agricultural College, where I purchased a pedigree Arab mare. Over the next nine years I reared nine foals and sold all but the last one for good prices. The last one I named *Ein Od*, which is the Hebrew for 'no more'!

As well as rearing horses, I came across a company for sale which made tree plates. When trees are heavily laden with fruit, the branches spread and droop to the ground, and can break without support. Earlier we would prop up the branches with limbs cut from saplings, but these were later replaced by wire. We would support the branches by tying heavy gauge wire around the circumference of the tree about two and a half metres from the ground. So that the wire did not cut into the branches, we would insert metal plates between the wire and the branches.

I bought the tree plate company and began operating out of a shed on our property. I did reasonably well for about three years, but the metal plates were then replaced by plastic and I closed down the business.

As we had also had experience in dehydrating fruit during the war, I had the timber mill make trays so that we could resume drying fruit in the sun. I started in a small way by buying apricots from neighbouring orchardists and drying them for my extended family. As I processed the apricots so that they would be kosher for *Pesach* and had more fruit than the family needed, I took the remainder to shops in Melbourne which sold *Pesach* goods. As the demand outstripped my supply, I prepared to dry as much fruit as possible the following year.

I knew a large packing shed which handled large quantities of apricots, so I began purchasing their apricots that were too ripe to send to the market. We then cut the fruit by hand, spread it out on trays and put it into a chamber which burnt sulphur to preserve the apricots. After eight hours in the chamber, they were spread out in the sun to dry, then packed into specially printed cellophane bags.

When you are dependent on the weather, things often happen that are beyond your control. It was most important that the fruit be brought in if it rained, and the weather could change in the middle of the night. If it did, the ever-reliable Angelo would come and wake me, as two people were needed to stack the heavy trays of fruit and cover them with a sheet of iron.

We produced a tastier, more appealing product than the larger manufacturers, who halved the apricots by machine, so they had to use firmer fruit, which was not as sweet. I continued this venture for ten years, doing very nicely from it until the orchards were sold.

Another venture was the gathering of palm fronds and *lulavim* – the young palm fronds in the centre of the trees which are not easy to reach – for the festival of *Succoth*. A few weeks before *Succoth*, I would drive my truck with the power ladder, taking a carload of workers to the areas I knew. The banks of the Murray River had many palm trees and Sepplets Winery in Barooga also had palm trees which I had permission to cut. I even went as far as Leeton in New South Wales. We would leave at daybreak and come back at nightfall and I would then deliver the palm fronds to Melbourne by truck. My brother-in-law sold them and remunerated me fairly for my efforts.

They say that those who plant pears plant them for their heirs, but not so with peaches. Peaches produce satisfactorily for twenty-odd years, but then they go backwards very fast and need new soil to grow. In California, where peaches are grown in much larger quantities, the soil is many metres deep and special machines are used to bring the deeper soil up so that the peaches have the fresh soil they need.

In Cobram, once the peach trees had been there for twenty years, the only alternative was to look for a replacement. Granny Smith apples were then the go, but many thousands of trees were needed to replace the peach trees. To buy thousands of Granny Smith apple trees from the nursery was very expensive, so I decided to try to grow them myself.

Growing a Granny Smith apple tree is a time-consuming business. In the first year you have to plant seeds and grow seedlings; in the second year you have to bud the seedling stock; then in the third year you have to make sure that only the bud grows, as that is what becomes a tree.

You may think that the stock grown from Granny Smith seedlings should yield Granny Smith apples, but this is not the case. If you do not bud the stock, the apples which grow could be any variety, either known or unknown. To bud the stock, the Granny Smith bud is inserted into the main stem of the seedling. The bud is taken from healthy trees which grow good quality fruit. Once the bud has grown, you then lift the tree and plant it in the orchard.

So, off I went to the juice factory to purchase the seed for the Granny Smith apples used for juicing. Three year later, we had trees for planting in our orchards, as well as a surplus of stock which I sold to the nursery. Despite our success, this venture was time consuming and labour intensive; we did not repeat it.

* * *

About ten years ago, the family met to decide whether or not to continue with the orchards. By that stage, most of my brothers had passed away and their descendants were involved in making decisions about the business. Half wanted to sell and the other half did not. We finally decided that we would not make a final decision for another three years. During that time, it was agreed that I would continue to run the orchards as if they were my own, sustaining any losses and keeping any profits. Although it was a risk on my part, I did very well, as evidenced by the large tax bill I had to pay!

The first thing I did as my own boss was to upgrade our equipment. I was interested in buying power ladders as I felt that our workers expended too much energy in the orchards going up and down ladders and wanted them to be able to concentrate on pruning. I phoned Ray Booth, the manager of Parsons Pty Ltd in Mooroopna, who had two power ladders left, so I asked that they be delivered to our properties in

Cobram. He promised we would have them in two days and refused my offer to pay, as he felt my word was good enough. Ray delivered the power ladders on the appointed date, set them up and came back the next week for his cheque. The resultant saving of labour more than made up for the cost.

* * *

I have mentioned the people who worked for us throughout my story, but it would be unfair if I did not do justice to the permanent staff who worked for us, both at Cobram and Shepparton.

You may have gathered that Angelo Michelin was a key person in the running of the orchards in Shepparton, but how he came to work for us is a story in itself! Angelo's cousin was a Coladetti and I had gone to school with three Coladetti siblings. Angelo had been a prisoner of war during World War II and had returned to Italy on his release. The Coladettis in Shepparton then sponsored him to come to Australia. My former classmate came to see me one day to ask me if I could give Angelo a job. I said I did not have anything available, but she came back a second time. Again I said no, as I did the third time. The fourth time she came, it so happened that we were about to plant pear trees and I was able to give him a few days work.

His cousin would have been happy for Angelo to work without pay as a trial, but I did not think this was fair. He began by helping us to plant the orchard and I could immediately see the calibre of the man. Not only was he practical, but he had brains and could have succeeded at anything if he had had an education. He turned out to be a real asset on the property and he retired thirty-four years later!

When Ruth and I and our family moved from the cottage into the house, Angelo and his family moved into the cottage so that we became neighbours. As well as working together we became best of friends, spending time together in the evenings. I felt I could discuss any problem with him and he would always help me find a solution.

Angelo was caretaker of the property throughout his working years. We charged him five shillings (fifty cents) a week rent and what a wonderful job he did in looking after things! Eventually he built himself a beautiful home in Shepparton, where his widow and daughter, Josie, now live.

In Cobram, two brothers came to work for us as lads of fifteen and sixteen years old. Their names were Laurie and Mervan Smith and they were loyal employees. Both were so reliable and capable that when we sold the orchards, the purchaser asked me to speak to them so that they would stay on. They agreed on condition that the new owner treated them as well as we did. Both went on to manage orchards.

In Shepparton, George Norton, like Angelo, also gave of his best and made my work ever so much easier. In 1999, my final year of running the orchards, Angelo sadly passed away. I had to go to hospital in Melbourne, so George put his shoulders to the wheel and did a sterling job running the orchards until I was able to return to work.

I also had a secretary called Judy Leerson, a country girl who was capable, hard working, pleasant and reliable. She put all her energy into whatever was needed – office work, light housework and supervising the packing of fruit for the market, a job she did for many years. The biggest problem was having to tell her to ease up and not work too hard. She came to work for us when my father was still commuting with me from Melbourne and he taught her how to keep things kosher so that she could prepare the vegetables for our dinner. I dare say she would probably know how to run a kosher kitchen better than many Jewish women!

Picking *lulavim* and *schat* for *Succot*
on the banks of the Murray River

In Ruth's own words

I have told you something about my background, my family and my work, but I would not be here telling you my story without the help and support of my wife, Ruth. Before I end my story, I think it is fitting to let Ruth tell you more about her life up till the time we met in London, so that our children, grandchildren and great-grandchildren have a more complete picture of their origins. So, it is with great pleasure that I hand over to her.

* * *

I was born in Zywiec, Poland, on 31 July 1927 and I was named after my late grandmother on my mother's side. My given name was Rochel bat Chana (Rochel, the daughter of Chana) but one of my mother's friends said that it was a very old-fashioned name and suggested I have the modern Hebrew name of Ruth instead. So Ruth it became!

My mother, Chana Rotter, was born in Zywiec in 1896. She was one of seven children: four sisters and three brothers. Her parents and grandparents also came from Zywiec. My maternal grandparents had a grocery store. At that time, people tended not to travel unless it was necessary to earn a living.

My father, Simcha Kanarek, was born in Bochnia, around one hundred and twenty kilometres from Zywiec. He was the same age as my mother. He was one of ten children, whose father sat in the *Bet Midrash* learning, while his mother was responsible for earning the family's finances, as well as bringing up the children. There was no financial aid, but my grandmother was a very resourceful person. She would buy eggs and store them in the cellar to sell during the winter at the best price she could obtain. Even so, it was very difficult to support such a large family, so my uncle and father left school at twelve to do whatever jobs they could find to help their mother. They would deliver groceries or messages, handing over whatever *grosz* they could earn so that my grandmother could buy food. My father always had a great ambition to study, but the family's financial situation meant that he was never able to realise his dream. The family never had new clothes, but my grandmother would remake clothes to pass on to the younger children. How she managed I don't know!

My parents met in Zywiec in 1916. Both were twenty years old. Because World War I was raging, my grandparents ruled out any possibility of marriage. During that time, men were being taken off the streets and conscripted into the army, regardless of capability or physical strength. My father continued to help his mother support the family and managed to evade the army. He and my mother began to correspond. I was aware of their love story because, as a child, I saw my mother's collection of my father's letters, tied together in bundles with different coloured ribbons for the different years. I'm not sure if I was allowed to read these letters, but I did!

Anti-Semitism was unbearable for the Jewish community and Zywiec was unique at that time as the only town to forbid Jews to live wherever they wished. Forced to live on the outskirts of the town, the Jewish people kept very close to each other, as it gave them a certain strength in those uncertain times.

After the war, my father continued to help his mother to support the family, but as his relationship with my mother became more serious, my parents looked for a place to live so that they could marry. It was almost impossible to find accommodation to rent after the war, but they finally found a place – a bedroom and kitchen – in 1921. My mother's father then took my father into his business and gave my parents permission to marry.

My sister, Bayla, was born in 1922; my brother, Moishe, in 1924; and I was born three years later.

My grandmother passed away the year before I was born so we moved into my grandparents' house and my parents looked after my grandfather. The poverty in the Jewish community of Zywiec was very great, but my family made enough to live on and were considered to be comfortable. My mother and father worked together. The house had a shopfront on the street and we lived behind the shop.

When my father took over the shop, he began to sell materials instead of groceries. On market days, after the people who had come to town from the surrounding countryside had sold their produce, they would come to our shop. We were extremely busy then and we would help our parents in the shop. It was my job to keep watch to make sure that no-one stole anything.

The shop was open for very long hours and my parents worked every day except Saturday. Although the government forbade trading on Sundays, the townspeople would come to the shop after they had been to church. As it was illegal to trade, our customers could not come into the shop from the street, but would come around the back and through the house.

Our house was quite small, but we had two bedrooms, a dining room and a kitchen. We had no running water, but we had a well and we had a live-in help who brought the water in from the well. A wooden stove burned around the clock. When we children were small, we shared a bedroom, but later my brother slept on a couch in the dining room and my sister and I stayed in the bedroom. The maid slept on a folding bed in the kitchen.

My mother employed a dressmaker once a month, mostly for making over old clothes so we could keep on wearing them. My sister's clothes were handed down to me and the only time I had a new dress was when I was twelve years old, for *Shavuot*. It was May or June and still quite cold, so I had to wear a coat, but I walked along the street holding my coat open so everyone could see my dress! The only things we could not hand down were shoes, so they had to be new. We always had something new – even if it was made over – for *Pesach* and *Rosh Hashanah*.

There were no buses or trams in Zywiec and we walked everywhere. If we went out of town on an excursion, we would hire a *fiacre*, a small horse-drawn carriage. Owning a car was very unusual and a sign of great wealth and we knew one Jewish woman, a doctor, who not only had a car, but also had a chauffeur as well!

Whilst a huge proportion of the Polish population was uneducated, the Jewish community placed high importance on education and there was no such thing as illiteracy, even if people only learnt Hebrew or Yiddish. Although the Jewish community lived on the outskirts of the town, the Jewish day school we attended was on the other side of town. In order to get from our home to school, we had to go in groups, as we were always harassed. Polish children, older than we were, threw stones at us or snatched Jewish boys' caps and threw them into the gutter. I grew up being frightened and constantly keeping watch for anyone who might harm us.

The school had six primary and two secondary grades. Jewish children who wanted to continue learning either had private lessons or learnt a trade. There were very strict quotas for Jewish children attending high schools and universities. Perhaps only one in twenty was able to go to local high schools. To make it more difficult, Jewish children were forced to attend school on *Shabbat*, which immediately excluded those from observant families. My brother wanted to become a dentist, so he had private lessons until World War II broke out.

I enjoyed learning and was a good student, unlike my sister, who was mischievous and always got into trouble. One time the children, who didn't like their teacher, decided to do something about it. They put a live mouse in a chocolate box, wrapped the box up with a ribbon and left it on the teacher's desk, which was on a podium at the front of the classroom. The teacher came in and smiled at the children when she saw the beautiful box. One of the children told her it contained a surprise and when she opened it, the mouse ran out. The teacher was so scared that she jumped up on the chair. The headmaster came and nobody would own up to the deed; finally they came to the conclusion that it must have been my sister's idea. My parents punished her by taking away her new navy blue school smock with a white collar and making her wear her old smock. They also took away her special earrings which had a little blue flower. I was not impressed by my sister's behaviour.

I loved school and was good at my schoolwork. My parents spent time helping me, my father concentrating on arithmetic. He would test my sums so that I knew them off by heart, drilling me constantly so that I could work things out quickly. My weakest subject was drawing, but I was good at writing stories. Luckily I made friends with one of the boys who was excellent at drawing, so I wrote and he illustrated my stories. As a result, we both got very good marks.

Although my parents were very busy, we always spent time together on *Shabbat.* This was a special time for the family and we always had special food. Although my mother worked in the shop, come Thursday evening she worked in the kitchen until the onset of *Shabbat.* She would be *kashering* the meat and chickens on Thursday evening, then get up at four o'clock on Friday morning to make *challahs.* She made so many that she had to take them to a commercial bakery for baking, as she had to use her stove for other dishes. She then cooked fish, chicken and compote. She even made her own wine out of raisins, which she boiled every week. On Friday night we ate the food my mother had prepared, but my father was in charge, singing *zmires* and making sure we all knew the words.

It was not until many years later, until I had my own children, that I was able to reflect on my own upbringing and realise what a wonderful relationship my parents had. I grew up in a home where my father and mother never argued. Obviously they must have had differences of opinion, but as children, we never heard a cross or impolite word between them. If I wanted something – a new hair ribbon, for example – I would go to my mother and ask for the five *grosz* it cost. If my mother said no, I knew there was no point in going to my father and vice versa. When I was eight, I wanted a doll, as I had never owned one, but when I asked my father he said no. However, I did not feel any resentment and still have beautiful memories of my father coming home from Cracow and Lodz with a special gift for my mother. He travelled regularly to buy materials for the shop and never came home without a gift for her – usually the newest and best quality fabrics.

My parents were such giving people and I have many beautiful memories of them. When my mother cooked for *Shabbat,* more than half of what she produced went to poor people. They came regularly on a Friday and she gave cooked food to some; to others, money or clothes we could no longer use.

As the 1930s progressed, anti-Semitism became much worse. At that time, Jews made up four million of the total Polish population of thirty-two million. I remember one of the first things the Poles did around 1937 was to forbid *shehita*. In 1938, Germany expelled Jewish people whose parents or grandparents originally came from Poland, and sent them to Poland. My mother took in two Jewish girls who had nowhere else to stay. They worked as helpers to a dressmaker, finishing clothes by hand.

I remember conversations in our house about whether to stay or leave Poland. Some of my parents' friends thought we should leave and others were adamant that we should stay. Those in favour of staying felt that as Hitler was uneducated

141

and had got rid of all the intelligentsia, apart from those who were willing to do his bidding, he would never amount to anything.

My parents chose to stay in Zywiec, although many others we knew left. Leaving was not easy, as you had to pay the government huge amounts of money. To do this, you had to sell whatever property and goods you had, just to cover the expenses, and most people were not rich to start off with. And, to go to England or America, you had to know someone there who could act as a sponsor and send money, and few people we knew had those kinds of contacts.

My school year finished in June and the war broke out on 1 September 1939, before the new school year began. At six o'clock in the morning, we heard the news on the radio that Germany had invaded Poland and my parents decided that we had to get as far away as possible from the Germans. We immediately packed whatever belongings we could take and went to the station. Whatever happened, my parents were adamant that we all had to be together, so the five of us boarded a train and went to Bochnia to stay with my paternal grandmother. My grandfather had passed away in 1938. We stayed overnight, but left at four o'clock the next morning to take a train going further east to Lvov.

The train was full of people, Poles as well as Jews, all running away from the Germans. Before we reached Lvov, the Germans began bombing our train. It came to a halt and we jumped out, rolling down the embankments on either side of the railway line. I was frightened but, more than anything, I remember my parents making sure we all stayed together.

We escaped from the train with nothing other than the

clothes we were wearing. When the bombing stopped, we started walking. We didn't know which direction to go, but someone directed us to the nearby town of Jaroslaw. The townspeople had gone into hiding in the surrounding forests and their homes were empty. It was *Rosh Hashanah* and there were enough Jewish people to make a *minyan,* so we decided to stay, as we thought we would be safe from the Germans.

During the week, while we were standing and praying, the door suddenly opened and the Nazis came in. They told us, in German, that we had to stop everything as we were under arrest. My brother tried to jump out of the window, but he was caught as he was opening it. They were ready to shoot him, but my mother, who had been educated in German, begged them not to. I still remember her telling them that although he was tall, he was only a young boy of fifteen. They were impressed by my mother's beautiful German and although they repeated that we were under arrest and must stay where we were, they left.

We stayed in that house for a number of days, living on the food the occupants had left. There were lots of chickens and I also remember swallowing raw eggs. The Nazis did not return and, a few days later, Germany and Soviet Russia agreed to partition Poland so half would be under German rule and the other half under Russian rule. As we happened to be on the Russian side, we were able to continue travelling and went to Lvov.

In Lvov we had to register with the Russian authorities, who recorded our personal details, including our religion. We were then allocated a room, for which we had to pay. This also entitled us to use space in a kitchen, which had one gas ring. Another two people – Mr Shtappler, a widower, and his unmarried son from Cracow – had to share our room.

We were in Lvov until July 1940. During that time my father found some odd jobs, but the money he earned was not enough to live on. My parents still had some Polish currency, so my mother was able to buy some dried beans and rice, which she sold to supplement his income. Without any warning, however, the Russians decided that Polish currency could no longer be used. Somehow my father managed to obtain some roubles, although how he did, I don't know.

All Polish citizens, both Jewish and non-Jewish, had the option to become Soviet citizens. This was supposed to come with all kinds of privileges, like work and money, but my father and hundreds of others refused. They were even called to see the police to coax them into accepting. Then we heard that the authorities were picking up males and sending them to Siberia. As a result, my father and brother and the young man sharing our room went into hiding in the cellar of our building.

In July 1941, at two o'clock in the morning, the Soviet authorities knocked on our door to tell us we had to go to Russia. When nobody moved, one of them said that just the men had to go, but they had to go immediately. My mother told me quietly to slip out of the room and tell my father. The men came up from the cellar and my mother grabbed my father's sleeve, telling him we could not be separated. My mother probably thought that we would all be shot right there, but we were told that we could stay together and all go. Mr Shtappler also decided to come, but he was told he was too old, and his son somehow disappeared. We never heard of them again.

We were taken to the station and put into cattle cars. There were benches in each car and by the time we left, our car was packed with sixty-five people, each with just enough room to sit. In the middle was a hole which everyone had to use a toilet. There was no privacy at all and it was horrendous.

We were not told where we were going and it was ages before we were given water or anything to eat. Every twenty-four hours each person was given a portion – *payot* in Russian – of food and water. The food was almost-inedible bread. We were not allowed to get off the train during our journey and we must have travelled for three to four weeks before we finally reached our destination. It was not Siberia, but somewhere a few hundred kilometres north of Moscow.

The train finally stopped in a clearing in the middle of a large forest and we were told to get out. We had arrived at a labour camp. The camp consisted of wooden barracks, with some kind of stuffing to fill the gaps between the logs. The wood was completely infected with bugs. Men and women were all housed together. This time we had nine people in our room – our family of five and a non-Jewish woman and her three children, also from Poland. The room was bare and the space was so cramped that we had to sleep legs to head on the floor so that we could fit. If someone wanted to get out, the person next to the door had to get up so that the door could be opened.

There was a communal kitchen and we were given rations of what was supposed to be vegetable soup every day. My age group was given lessons in Russian, which I enjoyed, and I picked up the language quite easily. In the afternoons I was free. My mother had not been mobilized to work like the men and teenagers, as she had a stiff hip, so she stayed at home.

My father, brother and sister had to work in the forest, chopping wood and sawing the logs. They worked twelve hours each day. In the afternoons, I was sent into the forest to pick mushrooms, wild raspberries, blackberries and anything else that was edible. We learnt very quickly which plants were edible and which were poisonous and there were lots of good mushrooms which grew until the onset of winter.

We soon found out we were in Maraiskaya. We were able to post letters, which we would give to the guards. Some letters were sent and others were not, but we were able to send my grandparents our address and ask them to send us parcels. We did receive parcels of clothes from various relatives, so my mother would give me an item at a time to trade with villagers for food. Children like me were sent out alone to the villages several kilometres away from the camp. Sometimes I would be lucky and would end up with a whole bucket of potatoes and somehow or other my mother managed to cook them. She had some kind of dish in which she could boil them on a crude stove made out of bricks. You could not live on the ration of soup provided to us, so these vegetables cooked in water were a real feast!

We spent close to two years in Maraiskaya. As the Germans were advancing, the Russians then decided that we had to be moved to Astrakhan, a port on the Caspian Sea. We travelled by boat down the Volga River without any food, but every now and then villagers on the banks would throw us some watermelon, which we shared around. It was another difficult trip which took about a week.

Again we were allocated to crowded rooms and the only food we were given was our daily ration. This was four hundred grams for people who were working, but for people who weren't, like my mother and me, it was only two hundred grams. Many fish were caught in the Caspian Sea and my father, sister and brother were sent to work in the fisheries where the fish was canned. If they were lucky, they could steal a fish and if they did, then I was sent to the market to exchange it for other food. I was very lucky that I was not caught, as the punishment was to be sent to Siberia. We heard of others who died on their way, or did not survive their time there.

Time passed and once again we were taken out of our camp and sent further away, this time to Kazakhstan. While not as far north as Siberia, it was close to the Chinese border. The camp was on the outskirts of a town and again the living conditions were horrific, with nine people to a room. And again the work was cutting down trees in the forest.

By that time I was old enough to go to work. As I had learnt to knit, I volunteered to work in the knitting factory which was nearby. Although I knitted for twelve hours a day, this was seen as easier work than labouring in the forest, which my father, sister and brother had to do. We mainly knitted socks for the Russian soldiers. My mother was quite unwell, so whilst the rest of the family worked, her task was to try to make a meal of any food we could steal.

Life was seen as very cheap, and if a tree fell on a worker in the forest, that worker was left to die. One day, my brother came back from work to tell us that he wanted to enlist in the Polish army that the Poles in Russia were forming within the ranks of the Russian army. When my mother heard the word 'army', she was very distressed. However, my brother argued that as we only had a fifty-fifty chance of survival where we were, he would not be any worse off if he joined, even knowing that he would be taken straight to the front. It was difficult for my parents to argue against this, so he enlisted.

At that time, my sister was ill so I had to go into the forest to help chop the wood. When I picked up the axe for the first time, I missed the wood and chopped into my hand. There were neither doctors nor medication, but there was a man with some basic medical knowledge who gave me a note to say I was unable to work. I was also unable to knit and I received a summons from the director of the factory to come and see him.

I spoke Russian well and the director was very friendly. He had invited me to see him to make me an offer. I would be given a special, warm jacket and trousers for winter and a new pair of shoes, as well as a double portion of bread and numerous other things. It sounded fantastic and as he was speaking, I sat there working out how I was going to distribute all these wonderful things! But then I asked what I had to do in return. His answer was that he wanted nothing more than for me to listen to what my parents and the others around me spoke about and let him know. This took my breath away and I stood up, telling him I would rather starve! I returned home and told my parents, who were very proud of me, and we all cried together.

Typhoid fever was raging in the camp and my sister became very ill. Many people died and as we all shared a very small room, we thought we would all be stricken. My sister was taken away to a hospital and although no one was allowed to go anywhere near it, I knew more or less where it was and managed to sneak in to see her. I went there each day with some food we had somehow managed to find, slipping in and out under constant fear of being arrested if caught. As her fever progressed, she lost consciousness, but two or three days later, the fever abated and she seemed better.

My sister's illness was terrifying and it affected her mentally, something I found very difficult to report back to my mother. My parents were told about a powder which may help, so I was sent to a nearby village to find it. I was allowed to leave the camp and as my arm was still bandaged, people were sympathetic. I managed to find the powder and gave it to my sister and it helped her regain control of her mind.

The war ended in 1945 and the Russians then decided to move us from Kazakhstan to Dniepopetrovsk. This time they put us in a *kolkhoz*; even though it had a different name, the conditions were just as bad as in the labour camps. By that stage, my sister and I were sharing one pair of shoes. We alternated from day to day, one wearing the shoes and the other wrapping her feet in rags. My job was to move wheat from one side of a storage shed to the other. I had to work for twelve hours a day, as did my father and sister. We were given half a day off, from seven until three o'clock, to celebrate the end of the war!

My brother wrote to us often, but we only received a letter from him every now and then. We also had what is known in Australia as the 'bush telegraph' – news would travel with people who were in some way connected; sometimes it was true and sometimes not. We did find out that he had met a Jewish doctor in the army who suggested that he become his aide. This not only gave him the opportunity to learn about medicine, but spared him from going to the front.

While I was working in the sheds, I would steal wheat by

hiding it in my shoes. We were searched when we finished our shift, so that was the safest place to hide it. My sister did the same when she was wearing our shoes. Someone had two stones with a handle to grind the wheat and the ground wheat was mixed with water. This extra bit of food helped to keep us alive.

In the winter of 1945, after the end of the war, we began to lose hope of ever leaving Russia. My brother had been able to go back to Poland and had received permission to bring the family back from Russia, but the Russian authorities kept postponing our departure. My brother was eventually allowed to come to Russia, so he came to rescue us in his Polish army uniform. As wonderful as it was to see him, it was also disheartening, as he was unable to do anything to influence the authorities.

It was impossible for just one family to leave and the authorities were not in a hurry to send back larger numbers, as we provided a source of unpaid labour. We were bullied by the guards and when I complained once that I was tired, I was told I should be grateful for the opportunity to work, as the alternative was death. At least during the war we used to have the hope of looking forward to peacetime, but now that the war was over, nothing had changed.

I believe that it was only because of my parents' unity and amazing strength that we all survived. Many years later, when the family was in Australia and my mother was unwell, she still kept telling us that we must always support each other, whatever differences we may have. This is something I hope I have imparted to my children as well.

One day, in February 1946, we were told to go to

Dniepopetrovsk. Once again we were put in cattle trains, but this time we were taken back to Poland. My mother managed to make what we called '*matzah*' for the journey – ground wheat mixed with water and baked over a fire. All the Russians did was supply each of us with a mug of boiling water when the train stopped at a station. Apart from our small supply of *matzah,* we had just the clothes we were wearing. The train trip took about ten days.

Arriving in Poland was horrendous. We went back to Cracow, where there was a larger Jewish population than in Zywiec. I was under no illusion that the anti-Semitism which had been there before the war would disappear, but I also did not think it could be worse – but it was! It was clear that the Polish people did not want the Jews to come back.

After some time, my father and sister went back to Zywiec to visit our property. One of my sister's friends came to meet them, crossed herself as if she had seen a ghost and warned them not to stay the night as they would not be safe. Apparently some Jewish people who returned and wanted to reclaim some of their possessions were shot during the night. My father and sister left and the family never returned to Zywiec.

My parents rented a room in Cracow. My father managed to sell our property in Zywiec at a very low price and this was all the money we had. As my brother had been a volunteer in the army, he was allowed to have one year of high school education. After passing his exams, he was able to go to university, so he went to Lublin to study medicine. He finished his medical degree, then went on to specialise in obstetrics and gynaecology.

My father, mother, sister and I lived a very frugal existence in Cracow. It was possible to cross the border illegally and go to displaced persons camps in Germany, Austria and Italy, but before this opportunity arose, Rabbi Schoenfeld arrived in Poland. He had collected large amounts of money from American and English Jews to take needy Jewish children to England, and one of those he had chosen was my cousin Shulamit.

By then we had been reunited with Shulamit and her father, Mendel, my father's brother, the only other members of our family who had survived the war. Mendel was managing to make money on the black market, buying and selling, as did many other people. Shulamit was eleven and had been in hiding during the war. As a result, she was unable to eat or dress by herself and had to be taken to the toilet, but her mental state was even worse than her physical problems.

As Shulamit was too ill to travel to England alone, my uncle suggested that it would be better for me to accompany her than for him to pay a carer to go with her. He felt that Shulamit would be better off in my care and it would also give me the opportunity to have a better life. After keeping the family together during the war, it must have been very difficult for my parents to let me go, but there was no life for Jews in Poland, and my parents wanted something better for me.

Shulamit had been living in a sanatorium, but my uncle brought her to our room and I looked after her for the few days before we left. I was nineteen and had no idea about looking after anyone with such disabilities.

I left Poland with only the clothes I had from Russia, as well as a scarf someone had given me. The youngest of our group was five and the oldest over thirty. We travelled by train from Cracow to Warsaw and then by aeroplane to Gdynia. We then boarded a ship which took four days to reach England. The weather was very bad and most of the children were very seasick. Luckily I was not and I was able to look after other children as well as Shulamit.

Before we disembarked, Rabbi Shoenfeld took the older members of the group aside and told us not to disclose our age as he only had landing permits for children up to the age of sixteen.

When we landed, we were welcomed warmly by a committee and taken to a hostel in London, where we were given two huge containers of second-hand clothes, one for boys and one for girls. There were so many clothes that we were all able to find things to fit. As there was only room at the hostel for the forty children that were expected, Rabbi Schoenfeld had made an announcement in his *shul* asking members of the congregation if they could take any of the children in, undertaking to pay for their keep. Everything was rationed in England at that time, but Rabbi Schoenfeld had a fantastic ability to raise money.

Taking on children and teenagers who had been traumatized during the war and who spoke only Russian, Polish or Yiddish was no easy task. Shulamit and I were assigned to stay with Mr and Mrs Deutsch, who lived at 13 Heathland Road, Stanford Hill. Mr Deutsch was German and Mrs Deutsch was Austrian. As I spoke German, we had no difficulty communicating with each other. They had one young child, a daughter called Judy, who slept in their bedroom, and Shulamit and I were given the second bedroom.

Mrs Deutsch's father had been the rabbi of a community

and had been given numerous chances to leave Austria before the war, but he would not leave until all the members of his community were safe. Rabbi Schoenfeld had come to the community in 1938, so that was how Mrs Deutsch was able to leave. She had trained in Austria as a kindergarten assistant and was able to work in London. Sadly, she was the only member of her family who survived.

The Deutsches were very welcoming from the minute we walked into their home and all these years later, Mrs Deutsch and I still speak to each other regularly. When I phoned her last *Rosh Hashannah*, she still referred to me as 'one of her children', even though she has four daughters and a son. Mr Deutsch was older than his wife and passed away some time ago, but Mrs Deutsch can't be much older than I am. I assume she was in her twenties when we met, and I was nineteen. It is only recently that I have begun to call her by her first name, Ilse.

Mrs Deutsch was, and still is, a truly amazing person. Mr Deutsch was also a fine person, but I was not as close to him, especially as he had a business in the West End, which meant that he was not around during the day.

As well as the money Mr and Mrs Deutsch received for our board, we were also issued with ration cards. I would give my ration book to Mrs Deutsch and she would give me my chocolate entitlement – a grand four ounces (one hundred and twenty-five grams) per month!

Rabbi Schoenfeld's father had established the Jewish day school movement in England, despite opposition from many English Jews who were proud of their school ties and did not want to be different from the general population. When

I arrived in London, Rabbi Schoenfeld ran a co-educational Jewish school called Avigdor High School. It was staffed by teachers whom Rabbi Schoenfeld had also rescued from Germany.

I was excited to be able to attend high school. There were eleven of us from the group Rabbi Schoenfeld brought from Poland and we made up one class. There were nine boys and two girls. The other girl was Toni Lublin, and she and I are still very close friends. She married a Londoner and they ran a kosher hotel in Golders Green before moving to Israel. Toni also brought her sister, who was deaf, to school. Although she could not speak, she was very bright and very good with her hands.

Shulamit attended kindergarten while I was at school. Our class was given English lessons while the others played sport or had music lessons. It took about six months until I was fluent enough to make myself understood and the first words I learnt were 'I don't understand English'.

In June 1946, at the end of our first term, Mrs Deutsch told me that Shulamit and I would have to move out of their home as she was expecting a second child and they would need to use our bedroom. Once again, Rabbi Schoenfeld found someone to sponsor us to move into an orthodox Jewish boarding school in Brighton, called Aryeh House. Most of the students were wealthy English and American children, as it cost around ninety pounds a term, an exorbitant amount of money in those days.

The funds to pay for that boarding school lasted for one term, so after that I moved back to London to rent a room in another boarding house. I was given a bed in a room which

I shared with two others, one of whom was the daughter of the owners and the other a refugee from Germany. Shulamit had to go to another boarding house, as there was no room for her to stay with me, and she was very unhappy. Luckily, when I met Aaron, her father came to London and she went to live with him. By that stage I had taught her how to eat and go to the toilet by herself, but she still needed help to bathe and dress.

We were given hot water and bread and margarine to take to our rooms and I would have this for breakfast and lunch. The only evening meal we were provided with was dinner on Friday night. On Saturdays, I would go back to the children's hostel I first stayed at for *Shabbos* lunch.

I realised it was time to find a job and earn some money, so Mrs Deutsch found me work as a machinist in a factory owned by a Jewish man. I had to learn to use an electric sewing machine, which only took me three or four days, and then I was given a job, earning two pounds two shillings a week (A$4.20). Out of my wages, I had to pay thirty-five shillings (A$3.50) for my board and the rest went on fares and living expenses, like shoe repairs and postage, so there was not much left for anything else. I still had the second-hand clothes I was given when I arrived in England and would repair them constantly so that they would last.

The boarding house was in the same street as the Deutsches so I would visit them often. At that time, I had very long hair which was difficult to wash so Mrs Deutsch helped me wash it at her place. As she was about to give birth to her second child, it was becoming a problem for her to help me. To complicate matters, water at the boarding house was metered and was expensive. I could afford the penny-halfpenny (less than A1.5 cents) to have a bath once a week and then use the same water to wash my clothes, but anything more was too expensive. To overcome the problem, Mrs Deutsch persuaded me to have a perm. I paid for it with the five shillings (A50 cents) pocket money Rabbi Schoenfeld allocated to his charges each week, supplemented by the few extra shillings I earned babysitting. The boys I knew were horrified when they saw my new hairstyle, but for me it made life a lot easier!

One day when I was visiting, Mrs Deutsch looked at my clothes and suggested I go back to the boarding house to change into something better, as a young man from Australia was coming for lunch. He was Moshe Feiglin's son, whom her husband had met at *shul* and invited home. So, I went back and changed.

I came back to the Deutsches and took Judy for a walk to meet her father while Mrs Deutsch was setting the table. This is how I first saw Aaron, although Mr Deutsch didn't introduce us. When we all came home, Mrs Deutsch introduced me to Aaron as 'Ruth Kanarek from Poland' and I left five or ten minutes later to go to the hostel for lunch.

I did not give my meeting with Aaron any more thought, but we saw each other again when he came back to London from Sweden in November. It was the night before Queen Elizabeth II (then Princess Elizabeth) was married and Mrs Deutsch had to go to the dressmaker by bus. As she was pregnant and did not feel comfortable going on her own, I offered to go with her. On the way back, we bumped into Aaron in the street and Mrs Deutsch could see that he was interested in me.

When Mrs Deutsch went to hospital to have her baby, Judy

was two, and I offered to look after her during the day. I took leave of absence from my job and spent each day there, taking care of Judy and doing the cooking. I would not accept any money and Mrs Deutsch was so grateful for what I had done that, with tears in her eyes, she said, 'For this I will take you under the *chuppah*.'

Aaron was living in a boarding house nearby and after our first couple of brief meetings, we would bump into each other in the street. Mrs Deutsch told me that he was very interested in me, but when she told him I was only sixteen, he thought that was too much of an age difference, as he was twenty-six. That is when I first told her that I was nineteen.

Mrs Deutsch immediately told Aaron to come straight over to her place and she told him that this sixteen-year-old was now nineteen! From then on we began to see more of each other. As he has told you, he asked me to go and see the film *Look Who's Kissing Her Now*, which was showing in the West End. It was my first date and I was very impressed, as the tickets cost four shillings (A40 cents). After catching the Underground back to Stanford Hill, we walked home and talked all the way.

I was not really interested in getting married, but Aaron told me all about his family and the businesses and properties they had in Melbourne and in Shepparton. As most of his brothers and sisters were in Melbourne and he also spent a lot of time there, I had no idea he intended to live in Shepparton. He painted a very happy picture of his life, especially to someone like me who had spent the war years without enough to eat. He also impressed my Uncle Mendel, so much so that my uncle wrote to my parents in Poland about him, describing the Feiglin family as *kmat ke*, (almost like) a Rothschild!

When Aaron suggested that we get married, I wrote to my parents to let them know and to ask for their permission. By then my parents were in a displaced persons camp in Milan. They were not happy with what I told them and my father wrote back immediately, asking how he could be sure that Aaron was Jewish and whether he was orthodox. My father also went to the Australian Embassy in Rome to find out the name of an orthodox rabbi in Melbourne. He was given Rabbi Gurewicz's name and sent him a telegram to try to find out something about the Feiglin family.

Rabbi Gurewicz sent a telegram back to my father confirming that there was a Feiglin family in Melbourne and that they were orthodox. Aaron's father also wrote my parents a beautiful letter in Yiddish, introducing himself and his wife and enclosing a photo of them with one of their grandchildren in their garden in Shepparton. After that, my father was reassured!

Aaron was anxious to return to Australia for the harvest and to see his mother, so we had very little time to ourselves before we married. As he has told you, our wedding happened very quickly and in just a few short weeks, I had arrived in Australia to start my new life there.

Looking back, almost sixty years later, I never would have dreamt of living on the other side of the world, let alone beginning my married life on an orchard in country Victoria.

Ruth, her Uncle Mendel and cousin Shulamit, Gdinia, Poland, 1946

Ruth's class at Avigdor High School, London, 1946.
Ruth is seated, far right

Epilogue

When Ruth and I were about to be married in London in 1948, we knew that my mother did not have long to live. My very good friend called me over and proposed that we go into business as equal partners. After thinking it over, I told him the next day that as much as I appreciated his offer, I would reluctantly have to refuse. I felt I could not disappoint my mother, who was waiting so patiently to meet her new daughter-in-law. My would-be business partner established a very successful business in London and became extremely wealthy in just a few years. Now, if anyone were to ask me if I regretted my decision, my answer would be 'not for a single moment'. As we all know, there is much more to life than money.

Very soon after we arrived in Australia, I was rewarded to see my mother and Ruth bond very closely with each other. My mother became Ruth's surrogate mother rather than her mother-in-law. She taught Ruth how to bake and cook, and imparted much wisdom to her. She was very taken by Ruth's fine character and dignity and she blessed her, telling her she would have orthodox children, both boys and girls. Sadly my mother's relationship with Ruth was far too brief, as she passed away less than two years after they met.

Having reached the twilight of our lives, Ruth and I look

back and tearfully thank the Almighty for the blessings that have been given to us in full measure. To see our complete extended family getting together and happily enjoying each other's company in good health is as much as one can wish for.

We see that our children have learnt from us what we have learnt from our parents; and our children, in turn, are teaching their children and their children's children.

Aaron with his oldest grandson, Zvi Trebish, Melbourne, 1981

Ruth and Aaron on their 40th wedding anniversary, 1988

Ruth and great-granddaughter, Sara Bella Kingsley, Melbourne, 2002

Aaron and Ruth with their children, grandchildren and great-grandchildren at granddaughter Blimi Ernst's wedding, Melbourne, 2006

Ruth and Aaron, Melbourne, 2007

Glossary

Affikomen	One of three pieces of matzah or unleavened bread, traditionally hidden and later retrieved and eaten at the end of the Passover meal
Bal Kera	Reader of the Torah
Berieh	Yiddish term of respect used for a capable housewife
Bet Midrash	House of study, place for the study of the Law and other texts
Bnei Akiva	Religious Zionist youth movement
Challah	Traditional egg loaf baked for the Jewish Sabbath
Chazen	(Hebrew: Hazzan) Cantor
Cholent	Slow-cooked stew of beef, beans and barley, traditionally prepared for the Sabbath
Chrein	Horseradish
Chuppah	Marriage canopy
Daven	Pray
Eierkichel	Sweet biscuits made with eggs

Grosz	Polish coin, 1/100 of a zloty
Kasher	Make kosher
Kiddush	Traditional blessing and prayer recited over wine on the eve of the Sabbath or a festival
Kolkhoz	Communal farm
Kreplach	Small dumplings of noodle dough filled with minced meat or cheese, usually boiled and served in soup
Kristallnacht	'The night of broken glass', a state-organised pogrom which took place throughout Nazi Germany on the night of 9–10 February 1938
Kugel	Baked pudding of noodles or potatoes, eggs and seasonings
Lokschen	Egg noodles
Lulav (lulavim)	Ripe, green, closed palm frond(s), one of the Four Species used in the daily prayer services during Succot
Maftir	Final section of the weekly reading of the Torah on the Sabbath and High Holy Day mornings
Matzah	Unleavened bread eaten during Passover
Mazel tov	Congratulations
Megillah	Scroll, or book; applied to the short books of the Torah, including the Book of Esther, basis for the Jewish festival of Purim

Melamed	Teacher
Minyan	Ten adult Jewish men required for communal prayer
Mohel	Jewish man qualified to perform ritual circumcisions
Parnosse	Living
Pesach	Passover
Prakes	Cabbage rolls
Rosh Hashannah	Jewish New Year
Shabbat/Shabbos	Sabbath
Simcha	Celebration
Shavout	Festival of Weeks, festival of the Counting of the Omer and the day the Torah was given on Mount Sinai
Shehita	Jewish ritual slaughter
Sheva broches	(Hebrew: Sheva berakhot) Seven benedictions recited at a Jewish wedding; also the festive meals in the week after the wedding
Shiva	The first seven days of mourning after a Jewish death
Shema Yisroel	'Hear O Israel', the first words of the prayer considered to be the most important in Judaism
Shochet	Jewish ritual slaughterer

Shofar	Ritual instrument made of ram's horn, usually used on Rosh Hashannah and Yom Kippur
Succot	Feast of the Tabernacles, a Jewish pilgrimage festival
Shul	Synagogue
Tallis	Prayer shawl worn by orthodox Jewish men during certain religious services and ceremonies
Teffillin	Phylacteries used by Jewish males aged thirteen and over for morning prayers
Tisha Ba'av	The Ninth of Av, an annual Jewish fast day
Torah	The Five Books of Moses, first five books of the Tanach, the Hebrew bible
Tzitzis	Fringes or tassels worn by orthodox Jewish men on the corners of four-cornered garments
Yid	'Jew' in Yiddish; can be used in a neutral or pejorative way
Yom Kippur	Day of Atonement
Yom Tov	Jewish holiday or festival
Zeide	Grandfather
Zmires	(Hebrew: Z'mirot) Sabbath songs